Cambridge Elements

Elements in Epistemology
edited by
Stephen Hetherington
University of New South Wales, Sydney

EMOTIONAL SELF-KNOWLEDGE

How Affective Skills Reveal Our Values, Goals, Cares, and Concerns

Matt Stichter
Washington State University

Ellen Fridland
King's College London

Shaftesbury Road, Cambridge CB2 8EA, United Kingdom

One Liberty Plaza, 20th Floor, New York, NY 10006, USA

477 Williamstown Road, Port Melbourne, VIC 3207, Australia

314–321, 3rd Floor, Plot 3, Splendor Forum, Jasola District Centre, New Delhi – 110025, India

103 Penang Road, #05–06/07, Visioncrest Commercial, Singapore 238467

Cambridge University Press is part of Cambridge University Press & Assessment, a department of the University of Cambridge.

We share the University's mission to contribute to society through the pursuit of education, learning and research at the highest international levels of excellence.

www.cambridge.org
Information on this title: www.cambridge.org/9781009494564

DOI: 10.1017/9781009307857

© Matt Stichter and Ellen Fridland 2025

This publication is in copyright. Subject to statutory exception and to the provisions of relevant collective licensing agreements, no reproduction of any part may take place without the written permission of Cambridge University Press & Assessment.

When citing this work, please include a reference to the DOI 10.1017/9781009307857

First published 2025

A catalogue record for this publication is available from the British Library

ISBN 978-1-009-49456-4 Hardback
ISBN 978-1-009-30784-0 Paperback
ISSN 2398-0567 (online)
ISSN 2514-3832 (print)

Cambridge University Press & Assessment has no responsibility for the persistence or accuracy of URLs for external or third-party internet websites referred to in this publication and does not guarantee that any content on such websites is, or will remain, accurate or appropriate.

For EU product safety concerns, contact us at Calle de José Abascal, 56, 1°, 28003 Madrid, Spain, or email eugpsr@cambridge.org

Emotional Self-Knowledge

How Affective Skills Reveal Our Values, Goals, Cares, and Concerns

Elements in Epistemology

DOI: 10.1017/9781009307857
First published online: June 2025

Matt Stichter
Washington State University

Ellen Fridland
King's College London

Author for correspondence: Matt Stichter, matt.stichter@gmail.com

Abstract: Knowledge of our emotional and bodily states helps us to further know our goals, values, interests, cares, and concerns. The authors first lay out a puzzle as to why bodily and emotional self-knowledge is strongly associated with good mental health and well-being. They solve this puzzle by mapping out connections between bodily states, emotional states, and our goals with an account of emotions as embodied appraisals. Emotions being embodied implies that self-knowledge of our bodily states aids in acquiring knowledge of our emotional states. Emotions as appraisals mean that situations are appraised relative to our goals, such that self-knowledge of emotional states aids in acquiring knowledge of our goals, which are not always transparent to us. While emotional self-knowledge can be difficult to acquire, through skilled practice we can improve awareness and knowledge of our emotional and bodily states.

Keywords: self-knowledge, affect, emotion, interoception, well-being

© Matt Stichter and Ellen Fridland 2025

ISBNs: 9781009494564 (HB), 9781009307840 (PB), 9781009307857 (OC)
ISSNs: 2398-0567 (online), 2514-3832 (print)

Contents

1 Introduction — 1

2 The Puzzle of "Feeling Well" — 4

3 Solving the Puzzle — 10

4 Emotions and Self-Knowledge — 20

5 Self-Knowledge Can Be Difficult to Acquire — 37

6 Conclusion — 56

References — 57

1 Introduction

"Know Thyself" – Temple of Apollo
"There are three things extremely hard: steel, a diamond, and to know one's self." – Benjamin Franklin, Poor Richard's Almanac

We think there are good reasons why the charge to "Know Thyself" has resonated so strongly through the ages. Having greater self-knowledge should be helpful for more effectively pursuing our goals and living in accordance with our most deeply held cares and concerns. Taking this as our starting point, we will go a step further by highlighting that an important and often overlooked type of self-knowledge is required for identifying our goals, values, interests, cares, and concerns, namely, emotional self-knowledge.[1] Emotional self-knowledge, as we understand it, is a kind of self-knowledge that provides us with knowledge of what we feel and is rooted in our ability to attend to and notice our own embodied emotional experiences.

Our interest in emotional self-knowledge stems in part from how it can make a significant practical difference in how our lives go. There's strong evidence that possessing emotional self-knowledge is associated with positive mental health and well-being, whereas a lack of it is associated with negative outcomes. However, there isn't a clear explanation of why that should be the case. We think trying to understand and explain that important aspect of emotional self-knowledge will provide us with a broader and theoretically rich account of self-knowledge, and so our project will be framed initially around the connection to mental health before drawing out the larger implications for self-knowledge.

In the following pages, we will clarify the nature and value of emotional self-knowledge by providing an account of emotion that makes it clear why attending to the body is key for acquiring emotional self-knowledge. This account of emotion holds that emotions are embodied appraisals, where those appraisals are based on our goals, values, interests, cares, and concerns (hereafter "goals+").[2] We will also suggest that such appraisals are rooted in interoceptive predictions of the body (and we mean this in the somatic sense of a "lived

---

[1] We hypothesize that one reason why emotional self-knowledge has been largely overlooked in philosophical discussions is because, typically, in the Western tradition, it is the rational or the cognitive that has been valued, exalted, and considered serious, scientific, and tough minded. Cassam notes a related point that irrationality often connotes emotionality (2014, 86). We hold that while cognitive judgments matter for guiding belief and action, affective and bodily appraisals matter too. Sadly, however, we have seemingly lost sight of the importance and the ability to acquire emotional self-knowledge and to use that knowledge as a guide, in a balanced and reflective way, to our goals, values, interests, cares, and concerns.

[2] This conception of a goal is meant to be quite broad in scope. For example, a goal can be short-term or long-term, can be a means to an end or an end-in-itself, and can be a "bucket list" item or an enduring standard one wants to live by (such as being an honest person) (Stichter 2018).

body"), which helps to explain the empirical evidence showing that the ability to detect internal physical sensations as well as the ability to identify and label one's own emotions in a fine-grained way are both systematically connected to mental health and well-being. Our focus will then be on the possibility of acquiring emotional self-knowledge via a skillful access to our own cognitive, affective, and bodily states.[3]

By way of background, we will mention briefly how our view connects to a current distinction in self-knowledge, but primarily we'll be pushing into some unexplored territory. Philosophical accounts of self-knowledge are concerned with having knowledge of one's own mental states. Knowing that you have a belief (e.g., you believe that it's raining outside), or that you are having a perceptual experience (e.g., you are seeing red), and so on would count as having "self-knowledge." For example, if I ask you whether it's raining outside, then I'm inquiring about the weather. But if I ask you whether you believe that it's raining outside, then I'm inquiring about your mental states. If you answer – "yes, I believe it's raining outside," then that is a claim of self-knowledge. One might draw a further distinction between "trivial" and "substantial" types of self-knowledge (Cassam 2014, 29). The reason for this distinction is that the aforementioned types of self-knowledge often seem "trivial" – both in content and in terms of how we come to know them. For example, coming to know that you have a belief that it's raining seems "trivially" easy to arrive at since it's just immediately known. It also seems "trivial" in its content, as it typically isn't practically useful for you to form a belief about whether you have the belief that it's raining. Insofar as you believe that it's raining, you'll act accordingly (e.g., you'll take an umbrella when you leave the house), and so what good does it do you to take that a step further and form the belief that you believe that it's raining?

Contrast that kind of trivial self-knowledge to knowing about your own abilities, attitudes, character traits, dispositions, emotions, goals, habits, and values. Quassim Cassam (2014, 30) claims that this latter kind of knowledge seems more "substantial" in a few respects, one of which is that it can matter in a more practical way given its content. We care about living according to our values, cultivating certain types of character traits, and achieving goals that are meaningful to us. Sometimes this is put in terms of living an authentic life or living up to our ideal selves. Having more substantial self-knowledge can be valuable in helping us to realize such aspirations. For example, if you're trying to become a more honest person, then it would help to know under what

---

[3] We view emotions as one kind of affective state, as there are other kinds of affective states (e.g., moods).

circumstances you might be prone to lying. Coming to know that about yourself could give you some insight into how to work on changing that aspect of yourself, to better embody your ideals. By contrast, trivial self-knowledge, such as knowing that you have a belief that it's raining outside, would rarely play such a useful role. Though, as Cassam rightfully notes, this distinction between trivial and substantial self-knowledge is likely a difference in degree rather than kind. But insofar as bodily and emotional self-knowledge is associated with mental health and well-being, we take it that our project will contribute to fleshing out accounts of substantial self-knowledge.[4]

In the sections that follow, we'll first elaborate on the idea that there's something puzzling about why self-knowledge of our bodily and emotional states should be connected to mental health in what we'll term the puzzle of "feeling well" at the start of Section 2, and then we provide empirical evidence of these connections (Section 2.1). In Section 3 we offer a solution to that puzzle by mapping out the connections between bodily states, emotional states, and our goals+ with an account of emotions as embodied appraisals (Section 3.1). Emotions being embodied means that emotional responses are accompanied by physiological changes which can redirect our attention and prepare us for action (Sections 3.2–3.4).

In Section 4 we argue that this view of emotion implies that self-knowledge of our bodily states helps us to acquire knowledge of our emotional states, and sometimes gives us insight into our goals+ as well (Sections 4.1–4.2). Furthermore, emotions being appraisals implies that situations are appraised relative to our goals+, such that self-knowledge of our emotional states helps us to acquire knowledge of our goals+ (Section 4.3). We further discuss some of the reasons why these types of self-knowledge are associated with good mental health and well-being, for example in aiding emotion regulation, having a better understanding of our cares and concerns such that we can set more appropriate goals, uncovering goal conflicts or goals that aren't transparent to us – such as in cases of outlaw emotions (Sections 4.4–4.6).

However, in Section 5 we also recognize that emotional self-knowledge can be difficult to acquire. Fortunately, there's evidence that through deliberate practice we can improve our awareness of our bodily states, which by itself improves our awareness of our emotional states (Sections 5.1–5.3), and that there are further ways we can practice to improve our emotional self-knowledge (Section 5.4). In doing so, we outline an account of skill that can usefully be applied to having skillful access to our bodily and emotional states. Finally, we

---

[4] Though we would classify our project in terms of "substantial" rather than "trivial" self-knowledge, nothing in our discussion that follows hangs on a defense of that distinction.

speculate that given that improvement in skill can lead to qualitative changes in how we interact with the world, we put forward the idea (along with some preliminary evidence) that becoming more emotionally skilled will lead to qualitative changes in our emotional experiences (Sections 5.5–5.6). Given that these are underexplored topics in discussions of self-knowledge, don't be surprised if we end up generating more questions than we answer!

2 The Puzzle of "Feeling Well"

It isn't hard to find imperatives in popular culture that encourage people to "feel your feelings" or to become more self-aware, accepting, and self-compassionate toward your own feelings and your "true self." These recent trends that advocate the awareness and acceptance of your own present moment embodied affective experiences (often called mindfulness) constitute the popularization of a growing consensus in clinical psychology that holds that practices of accessing, contacting, attending to, examining, noticing, tolerating, and soothing distressing emotions are key to mental health and well-being. After all, questions frequently asked by psychotherapists include: "how does that make you feel?" and "where do you feel that in your body?" Modalities in clinical psychology from Dialectical Behavioral Therapy (DBT) and Acceptance Commitment Therapy (ACT), and Mindfulness Based Cognitive Therapy (MBCT), so called "third-wave" cognitive behavioral therapy approaches to Internal Family Systems (IFS), Emotion Focused Therapy (EFT), self-compassion and trauma-informed interventions all have at their core a commitment to the idea that a sort of friendly self-knowledge of our own affective and bodily states is key to well-being and good mental health. As we'll review more later, the empirical evidence showing a positive correlation between interoceptive capacities, emotional awareness, and mental health seem to bear out these practices and commitments.[5]

However, the question remains, *why* would self-knowledge of our own feelings or emotions, occurrent affective and embodied sensations, have this effect? It is to our knowledge still unexplained why knowing what feelings we are feeling and, more specifically, how we are feeling those feelings *in our bodies,* should lead to more positive well-being. After all, why should knowledge and acceptance of our own interoceptive and affective sensations be so central to mental health? And why should knowledge concerning one's own feelings or experienced emotions be particularly impactful for our mental health

---

[5] It's worth noting that "conscious feelings are not required to produce emotional responses, which, like cognitive processes, involve unconscious processing mechanisms" (LeDoux 2000, 156–157), and so "[f]eelings can be regarded as states of emotional consciousness, bearing all the relevant characteristics of conscious states" (Taylor & Fragopanagos 2005, 354).

in general? It seems obvious that controlling or regulating emotion-fueled behavior is connected to greater well-being and higher social functioning, but why is being better at detecting one's own emotions and internal sensations in the first place so important? That is, why is emotional self-knowledge, in and of itself, important for overall well-being? It seems that Mary might not know what it is like to see red but can still be a well-adjusted scientist. Empirical evidence and clinical practice seem to suggest, however, that if Mary doesn't know what it is like for her to feel sadness *in her body*, she may be prone to a variety of mental health challenges. But, for reasons we'll outline next, clinical psychologists mostly take this fact as given and so do not provide a robust theoretical explanation for why acquiring emotional self-knowledge should lead to better mental health and well-being outcomes.

We might then turn to philosophical accounts of self-knowledge to provide an explanation of the connection between emotional self-knowledge and mental well-being. But, despite the fact that in corners of philosophy, psychology, and the cognitive sciences there is consensus about the fundamental interconnection, or perhaps even an interdependence, between cognition and emotion (Bechara et al. 2005; Colombetti 2020; Colombetti & Thompson 2007; Damasio 1999; Maiese 2014; Prinz 2004; Shargel & Prinz 2018), when it comes to philosophical discussions of self-knowledge the focus of inquiry is almost entirely on propositional states as an isolated category of knowledge. Emotional and bodily states receive significantly less attention than cognitive ones. While it's acknowledged that one type of self-knowledge we could have is knowledge of our emotional states, it's typically considered just one more potential object of self-knowledge among many, and is not usually thought to be necessarily connected to other valuable states such as good mental health and well-being. This may be due to emotional states being considered irrelevant or irrational and, as such, either ignored or viewed as problems that need to be overcome. So, this means that a thorough exploration of the nature, value, and acquisition of emotional self-knowledge is missing from the philosophical literature.

Thus, the puzzle of "feeling well" as we understand it is *why* it is that good mental health is to some extent dependent on having bodily/affective/emotional self-knowledge, and why a lack of such knowledge contributes to poor mental health and well-being. Since current theorizing in psychology and philosophy leaves this puzzle unresolved, we will attempt to provide a preliminary explanation for this connection. Moreover, we expect this explanation to also yield a more robust account of the nature of emotional self-knowledge.

2.1 Evidence of a Connection

Why think that greater emotional self-knowledge leads to better psychological, social, and physical health outcomes? You don't have to merely take our word for it, as there is a significant amount of empirical evidence for this connection. The evidence comes in the form of a double dissociation, which is the gold standard for causal inference, as there is evidence to support both the claims that greater emotional self-knowledge is associated with better mental health, and that less emotional self-knowledge is associated with worse mental health outcomes. In reviewing this evidence, we hope that it also serves to provide good reasons for why you ought to care about emotional self-knowledge (in case you didn't already).

One source of evidence comes from research on emotional differentiation and emotional granularity. Emotional granularity and emotional differentiation are often used interchangeably to refer to the phenomenon of differentiating emotional experiences with different fineness of grain. What's important to notice is that people differ in their ability to make such fine-grained distinctions concerning their own emotional experiences. That is, some people are high in emotional granularity and others are low (Barrett et al. 2001). People low in emotional granularity use diffuse, sweeping, general categorizations for their feelings, like "feeling bad" or "feeling good" while those high in emotional granularity can label their emotional experiences in a more precise, fine-grained fashion. For example, instead of identifying themselves as "feeling bad" people high in emotional granularity may be able to identify the bad feeling as an instance, say, of anger, nervousness, shame, guilt, or fear.

Crucially, people's abilities for emotional differentiation are positively correlated with important psychological, social, and health outcomes. For instance, people who are high on emotional differentiation have been found to drink less in stressful circumstances (Kashdan et al. 2010) and to be less likely to retaliate aggressively to a perceived injury (Pond et al. 2012). Additionally, people who are low on emotional differentiation are more likely to suffer from an array of mental health disorders (Kashdan et al. 2015), including depression (Demiralp et al. 2012), social anxiety (Kashdan & Farmer 2014), eating disorders (Selby et al. 2014), and borderline personality disorder (Suvak et al. 2011).

Another source of evidence comes from the burgeoning literature on interoception, which strongly suggests that there is a clear connection between emotional awareness, emotional regulation, emotional well-being and the ability to accurately detect and use information from internal bodily systems. Interoception refers to the detection and perception of internal afferent bodily signals (Craig 2003; Critchley & Garfinkel 2017; Khalsa et al. 2018).

Interoception is key to bodily homeostasis and occurs across all major biological systems, including cardiovascular, pulmonary, gastrointestinal, nociceptive, and visceral (Khalsa et al. 2018). Much of interoception occurs below the level of consciousness, but there are important interoceptive signals that can be detected subjectively by individuals, and these include but are not limited to heart rate, respiration, perspiration, flushing, fullness of the bladder, and gastrointestinal feelings (Khalsa et al. 2018). Such signals are often related to bodily states such as hunger, thirst, energy level, stress, desire, and pain (Fischer et al. 2017).

Additionally, a host of research now indicates that there is a substantive connection between the ability to detect interoceptive signals and awareness of one's own emotional states (Bechara & Naqvi 2004; Bornemann & Singer 2017; Herbert, Herbert & Pallatos 2011; Herbert & Pallatos 2012; Koch & Pollatos 2014). Accuracy in identifying internal bodily states is positively correlated with sensitivity to one's own and other's emotional states (Bird et al. 2010; Bornemann & Singer 2017; Terasawa et al. 2014). Furthermore, there is clear evidence linking interoceptive awareness not only to the ability to identify emotional states but also to regulating one's emotional responses (Barrett et al. 2004; Craig 2003; Herbert et al. 2011; Füstös et al. 2013). That is, "good interoceptive accuracy is generally associated with better affective regulation" (Critchey & Garfinkel, 2017, 11). For instance, individuals who have greater interoceptive awareness have been found to be better able to downregulate affect as well as to modulate concomitant neural activation using reappraisal techniques (Füstös et al. 2013). Interoceptive awareness has also been positively linked to intuitive decision-making (Dunn et al. 2010).

On the flip side, a host of evidence links disordered interoception with several psychopathologies. Interoceptive deficits have been linked to eating disorders such as anorexia nervosa (Khalsa 2015; Pollatos et al. 2008), depression (Furman et al. 2013; Pollatos et. al. 2009; Terhaar et al. 2012), mood and anxiety disorders (Domschke et al. 2010), substance abuse disorders, PTSD, and panic disorder (Ehlers et al. 1995; Khalsa et al. 2018 for review). In all, the emerging picture from interoception research clearly links interoceptive abilities to emotional awareness and regulation. Moreover, deficits in interoceptive abilities are linked to psychopathologies while better interoception is connected to better emotional regulation and emotional health.

Two further lines of empirical evidence help us to solidify a clear connection between disordered emotional awareness and poor mental health outcomes. One line of evidence comes from studies of alexithymia. Alexithymia is a subclinical concept or construct characterized by disrupted or diminished emotional awareness and is connected to numerous psychological and psychiatric disorders. Alexithymia refers to an "impaired ability to be aware of, explicitly identify, and describe one's feelings" (Hogeveen & Grafman 2021, 2). Importantly, alexithymia is characterized not only by an explicit linguistic or cognitive deficit but also by the tendency to "avoid internal, affect-related thoughts" (Hogeveen & Grafman 2021, 2). Alexithymia has also been shown to be associated with a number of mental health disorders, including major depressive disorder (Leweke, Leichsenring, Kruse, & Hermes 2012), generalized anxiety disorder, panic disorder, posttraumatic stress disorder (PTSD), and possibly obsessive-compulsive disorder (Frewen et al. 2008a; Onur et al. 2013; Shipko et al. 1983; Zeitlin & McNally 1993). There is also evidence of an association between alexithymia and addictive behaviors such as pathological gambling (Elmas et al. 2016) and addiction to substances (Betka et al. 2018; Stasiewicz et al. 2012). Furthermore, as Hogeveen and Grafman (2021, 4) describe, "[a] recent meta-analysis suggested that approximately 50% of individuals with autism spectrum disorder (ASD) meet criteria for comorbid clinically-significant alexithymia, roughly 10 times the rate in the general population" (Kinnaird et al. 2019). It is worth noting that alexithymia is a somewhat flexible measure in that individuals naturally vary in their emotional awareness abilities, but these abilities are not fixed. Rather, it has been shown that alexithymia can indeed improve with training. In one study, training in interoceptive body awareness was shown to lead to increases in emotional awareness and decreases in alexithymia (Borneman & Singer 2017).[6]

One other line of evidence for an association between poor emotional self-knowledge and negative mental health and well-being outcomes comes from research on experiential avoidance. Hayes et al. define experiential avoidance (EA) as a "phenomenon that occurs when a person is unwilling to remain in contact with particular private experiences (e.g., bodily sensations, emotions, thoughts, memories, behavioral predispositions) and takes steps to alter the form or frequency of these events and the contexts that occasion them" (1996, 1154). Of note is the fact that like the impacts of alexithymia, poor emotional differentiation, and low interoceptive awareness reviewed earlier, experiential avoidance is associated with many psychopathologies (Chawla & Ostafin 2007).

Finally, it is worth noting that a lack of contact with one's emotional experience is associated not only with but also with diagnostic of the presence of

---

[6] Given the decreases in alexithymia occurred after training in body awareness, we take this to provide evidence that self-knowledge in this case is having an effect on well-being (rather than the reverse relationship). Training in emotion differentiation and in affect labeling, which we discuss in later sections, shows similar patterns (though we leave it an open question as to whether the reverse relationship occurs in other cases).

psychopathology. This is evident from the fact that the *DSM-5* makes clear that PTSD is highly correlated with dissociative reactions. In fact, the *DSM-5* (2013, 272) lists several kinds of dissociative symptoms as characteristic of PTSD, including depersonalization, which involves "feeling detached from, and as if one were an outside observer of, one's mental processes or body (e.g., feeling as though one were in a dream; feeling a sense of unreality of self or body or time moving slowly" and/or derealization which is defined as "persistent or recurrent experiences of unreality of surroundings (e.g., the world around the individual is experiences as unreal, dreamlike, distant or distorted)." This class of reactions is often interpreted as a way of coping with the recurrent, involuntary, intrusive, and distressing memories connected to trauma. The disconnection from self and experience, however, often occurs in ways that generalize well beyond the specific memories of the trauma. In fact, the unwillingness or inability to feel what is going on for oneself and one's body is a pervasive and deeply unsettling reality that many sufferers of PTSD experience (Fisher 2019; Ogden, Pain, & Fisher 2006; Van der Kolk 1994). In this way, we see that disconnection from one's own experience, including the inability to embody and fully experience one's emotions, is not only correlated with negative mental health but is itself a symptom of a serious mental disorder.

At this point, we believe that we have provided sufficient evidence of a robust connection between emotional self-knowledge and mental health and well-being outcomes. Furthermore, this discussion should have served to provide us with some reasons to see acquiring emotional self-knowledge as valuable, at least insofar as it contributes to better mental health and well-being. Though we also want to emphasize that we do not take emotional or bodily self-awareness to be incorrigible or to never require correction *all things considered*. There are plenty of examples of people being mistaken in their beliefs about their own emotional or bodily states, or having emotional responses that are inappropriate or otherwise maladaptive in situations (and we'll go into detail about this in later sections). However, the fact that awareness based on affective and bodily information can go wrong is not by itself a reason to reject the utility and importance of such awareness. After all, we know that inference and rational beliefs often go wrong too and are notoriously susceptible to a whole set of cognitive biases, yet we do not dismiss them out of hand. In what follows, we will focus first on the functional role that affective and bodily self-knowledge plays in our lives to solve the puzzle of "feeling well."[7]

---

[7] It might help to note that our concern with knowledge of our bodily states is specific to those bodily sensations connected to affect, emotion, and our goals+.

3 Solving the Puzzle

We will argue that an important piece in the puzzle of why emotional and bodily self-knowledge should matter for mental health and well-being is that such self-knowledge is indispensable for knowing what matters *to us* – our goals, values, interests, cares, and concerns – what we like, what engages and excites us, what makes us feel alive and energized, what leaves us depleted and depressed. In this respect, we agree with Cassam that "feelings of joy, anguish, or suffering provide us with access to truths about ourselves which may not be accessible in other ways" (2014, 181). What remains to be spelled out in greater detail, of course, is why these feelings can provide access to truths about ourselves, what these truths might be, as well as why knowing these further truths about ourselves is beneficial to mental health and well-being. Just to be clear, our claim is that emotional and bodily states are inherently connected to our goals+ and, as such, present us with a distinctive pathway for acquiring knowledge of our deeply held values, priorities, cares, and concerns. In this way, emotional self-knowledge can help us to achieve better outcomes because of its instrumental value (e.g., usefulness for better self-regulation and more congruent goal setting). We also want to emphasize, however, the inherent value of emotional self-knowledge where such knowledge can become a transformative opportunity to experience oneself, one's relationships, and one's world differently.

3.1 Emotions as Appraisals Related to Goals+

In defense of the claim that emotions are inherently related to our goals+, we draw on multiple interdisciplinary perspectives on emotion that claim the two are tightly connected. For example, control theory and cybernetics seek to explain how goal-directed systems (e.g., humans, but also animals and machines) can use feedback to self-regulate their actions. Carver and Scheier (1990, 33) claim that emotions can play a role in self-regulation for:

> emotions intrinsically are related to goal values, and that they reflect differences between expected and experienced rates of movement toward (or away from) those goals. They represent an organismic monitoring of "how things are going" with respect to those values.[8]

---

[8] The reference to "differences between expected and experienced rates" foresees the role of expectations and prediction errors in shaping the emotional response. Regarding expectations, consider how our affective reactions to situations can also vary depending on our prior expectations (e.g., walking into a movie with low versus high expectations of it being good). Also, when expectations aren't met, this could be regarded as a prediction error, and such errors play a central role in current predictive processing models of the brain in cognitive science. Ridderinkhof (2017, 320), in a discussion of a predictive processing take on emotion in action, claims that with emotional appraisals of situations the "central appraisal is whether an event is assessed as

So, in this sense, emotions can provide us with feedback about whether our goals+ are being met or not, and we can take action in the light of that feedback. Also, this idea of an "organismic monitoring" is suggestive of the potential relevance of the body in emotional experiences (as we'll detail in the next section on emotions as embodied appraisals).

This connection between emotions and goals is also commonly endorsed in psychological theories of emotion, as Thompson et al. (2021, 8) have recently emphasized that:

> Multiple emotion models posit that emotions arise in situations that are relevant to the goals, needs, and concerns of an individual (e.g., Barrett, 2006; Frijda, 1986; Scherer & Moors 2019). Thus, in part, emotions indicate the extent to which goals are achieved (or blocked), needs are fulfilled (or neglected), and concerns are alleviated (or exacerbated).

Emotions thus involve appraisals of situations in the light of our goals+. Furthermore, Taylor and Fragopanagos (2005, 354), in a discussion of evidence in neuroscience that emotions guide attention, claim that "[e]motions and goals are strongly intertwined in the sense that the immediate relevance of any stimulus to a goal defines the emotionality of the stimulus." So, emotions can also play a role in drawing our attention to aspects of a situation because those aspects potentially support or thwart our goals, needs, or concerns.

Phan and Sripada (2013, 376) further elaborate on how situational appraisals are shaped by our goals+, including goals we're not consciously thinking about, in claiming that in the unfolding of an emotional process:

> the person engages in cognitive appraisals, which can be fast and automatic or slower, deliberate evaluations of how the situation relates to his or her goals (Ortony, Clore, & Collins 1990). These goals can be momentary or enduring; they can be held consciously with volitional intent or reflexively without awareness (Gross & Thompson, 2007). Specific emotions are then triggered depending on how the situation is appraised relative to the person's goals (e.g., fear is triggered if a core survival-related goal is threatened, anger is triggered if a goal is frustrated, and so on).

In sum, there is a significant scientific convergence on the idea that emotions involve appraisals of situations relative to our goals+ (i.e., whether the situation affords opportunities for them to be supported or thwarted).[9] Furthermore, it

---

promoting or obstructing one's concerns ... Concerns relate to norms, preferences, interests; to whatever affects the presence, availability, or intactness of everything the individual cares about."

[9] "Convergence," though, does not imply "consensus." However, we're taking this to be a very plausible and widely endorsed view such that we can use it as a basis for theorizing connections between emotion and self-knowledge (as it's beyond the scope of this manuscript to offer a new account of emotion).

would be hard to see how emotions could play a functional role in our lives if they were entirely divorced from our goals+ instead.

There is also a significant convergence in philosophical accounts of emotion that emotions involve evaluative appraisals. As Jean Moritz Müller (2017, 281) writes, "[m]uch current philosophical work on affectivity conceives of emotions as evaluations. A popular version of this idea has it that emotional evaluation is a form of epistemic access: emotions apprehend the significance or value of objects and events in our surroundings" (e.g., Tappolet 2000, Roberts 2003, 2013, Deonna 2006, Teroni 2007, Slaby 2008, Deonna & Teroni 2012, 2014, 2015).[10] The idea is that in feeling an emotion, one is detecting an evaluative property of an object, person, or situation at which the emotion is directed. For example, the emotional experience of boredom is how we detect the property of being uninteresting – that is, we evaluate, in a bodily way, the situation as boring when a situation is uninteresting. The emotional experience of sadness is how we detect loss, and the emotional experience of fear is how we detect danger (Prinz 2004). In this way, emotions are epistemically indispensable. As Deonna and Teroni (2022, 2) explain, the *Indispensability Claim* has been endorsed by many philosophers and amounts to the idea that "emotions are indispensable in acquiring knowledge of the relevant values" (D'Arms and Jacobson, 2010; DeSousa 1987; Goldie 2004; Johnston 2001; Tappolet 2016).

Although we agree that emotions can play this role in the acquisition of evaluative knowledge of things external to us, since we're looking to improve knowledge of ourselves, what we want to focus on instead is a different epistemic role for emotions in the acquisition of self-knowledge. For example, it might be that we notice our amusement in response to a joke but deny that it detects an actual feature of the world. It isn't, after all, too confusing to say: I know that the joke isn't funny, but it just cracks me up every time. Knowing what one feels, in this way, is not only important for detecting evaluative features of the world but for knowing how it is that one responds to the world that one navigates, whether or not one endorses a straightforward connection between emotional responses and accurate detection of normative properties.

We suggest that one main reason that self-knowledge of one's emotions (which are themselves embodied states, as we will discuss next) is crucial for

---

[10] While Müller (2017, 295) offers an alternative to appraisal theories in the form of a "Response View," he still views emotions as responses to a prior appraisal, and notes that as a result "it might be argued that the Response View at least entails a version of the appraisal theory," and that in any case "it is clear that the two approaches are closely related in that both start from the observation that awareness as of the significance of objects or events contributes to bringing about emotions and thus precedes them." See endnote 14 for related points.

well-being is because this kind of self-knowledge is indispensable for identifying *the value of the world for us*. Emotions reveal what matters to us and thus constitute a method for acquiring such critical self-knowledge.[11] Knowing how we feel in different situations, with different people, while engaging in different activities, and at different times is the only way we have for learning about the value that these different situations, people, and activities have *for us*. The claim we are making is that emotions are not only important for providing us with access to the evaluative or normative properties of the world, a claim that many philosophers have made,[12] but that self-knowledge of our emotions is necessary for knowing the value of the world *for us*, whether those evaluative properties of situations are ultimately accurately detected, endorsed, or rejected.

Emotions, though, are more than just situational appraisals connected to our goals, values, interests, cares, and concerns, for emotions are also intimately tied to our bodily and motivational states. So, exploring accounts of emotions as embodied appraisals will allow us to build on the earlier claims, as well as help us to provide an explanation for part of the puzzle as to why knowledge of bodily states is also connected to mental health and well-being. Our claim will be that self-knowledge of our bodily states is a route to better self-knowledge of our emotions because emotions are themselves best understood as embodied appraisals. Of course, knowledge of emotion, as we are claiming, is a route to better self-knowledge of our goals+, and this self-knowledge promotes adaptive responses, better health outcomes, and the possibility of transforming some of our most fundamental ways of being in the world.

3.2 Emotions as Embodied Appraisals

To see both why emotions can play the role of revealing the value *for us* of various objects, people, and situations, and to see why this detection of value is intimately tied to the *soma* or the lived body, it is useful to appeal to an embodied theory of emotion. In our view, that theory begins with an enactive view of emotion that has been forwarded by theorists like Michelle Maiese and Giovanna Colombetti. Enactive accounts of emotion as embodied appraisal can help to explain why attending to our bodily and affective states can give us insight into what we find meaningful, rewarding, and valuable. That is, these kinds of theories of emotion can help us to explain why attending to our bodies

---

[11] It's important to note that what we think emotions enable us to learn about ourselves are our current goals, values, interests, cares and concerns – as those are shaping how we're responding to the world. It will be a separate question as to whether we ought to preserve, revise, or reject those goals+.

[12] Deonna 2006; Deonna & Teroni 2012, 2014, 2022; Roberts 2003, 2013; Tappolet 2016; Teroni 2007; Slaby 2008.

is a way of accessing our emotions and thus revealing to us our values, priorities, cares, and concerns. To begin with, it's important to notice that almost all theories of emotion admit, to various degrees, that the body has some role to play in emotional experience. That said, of course, bodily perception theories in the tradition of James-Lang put the perception of bodily states at the center of their account of emotion (Damasio 1999; Prinz 2004), while cognitivist theories hold a more tenuous connection to the body (Nussbaum 2001; Solomon 1980). Still, cognitivist theories with their emphasis on judgment help us to see that emotions are indispensable for epistemic access to the evaluative features of the world. In this way, we are firmly committed to both bodily and cognitive elements of emotion. What we will try to show next is that because emotions involve changes to the body, attending to one's body is a way for us to come to know our emotions and, thus, what our emotions reveal to us: our values, cares, and concerns.

Our main contention is that better access to affective and bodily information is necessary for coming to identify our goals+. While this claim is compatible with a plurality of hybrid theories of emotion, we will draw specifically on Michelle Maiese's (2014) embodied appraisal theory since by her account it's explicit that emotional experiences not only depend upon but are, at least partially, constituted by the physiological changes characteristic of emotional states. This is consistent with findings in affective neuroscience that emotions "produce a coordinated suite of changes across multiple cognitive and physiological systems" (Phan & Sripada 2013, 376). That said, it's helpful to note that the claims we make could be partnered with a variety of hybrid theories of emotion that diverge in their details from the one that we rely on here.

According to enactivist accounts of emotion, the bodily and cognitive components of emotion are inseparable. Emotions are cognitive insofar as they involve embodied appraisals of situations (e.g., feeling fear indicates the situation is likely dangerous), and are felt in terms of bodily changes (e.g., increased heart rate, blood pressure, or sweating). Furthermore, as Maiese (2014, 519) points out, emotions aren't merely passive reactions to situations because embodied appraisals are "modes of responsivity that shape subsequent cognitive processing" and behavior. For example, feeling fear is likely to prime the body for a fight-or-flight response (and so this appraisal goes together with bodily changes), and will alter the way in which one pays attention to various features of a situation and how they will be assessed, for example, whether they are further indications of threat or safety.

Importantly, those appraisals are connected to our goals+. As Colombetti (2020, 52) has claimed, "emotions embody interests" and "an embodied interest, as an interest, reveals something about what the organism in question cares about." Insofar as our emotional responses are shaped in part by our cares and concerns, attending to our affective and bodily reactions not only give us information about what is significant in the environment but also provide us information about the content of our goals+. This becomes especially important when we realize that these cares and concerns shape our perceptions of (i.e., attention), and reactions to (i.e., preparedness), the situations we find ourselves in via emotion.[13]

3.3 Emotions Guiding Attention

One function of emotion is to change what we're attending to in our environment because of the presence of something that potentially supports or thwarts one of our goals, values, interests, cares, and concerns. Before discussing how emotions have this effect it will be helpful to make a few general points about the nature of attention, and this discussion of attention will be helpful later in explaining what we mean when we claim that it's important to attend to our affective and bodily states. As Wayne Wu (2011, 2024) in philosophy and Richard Krauzlis et al. (2014, 2023) in neuroscience have long argued, research on attention should be understood as an effect that we're trying to explain (rather than treating attention as a cause or explainer). Furthermore, they understand attention as an effect of processes that help us to select effective behavior. Krauzlis et al. (2021, 2, emphasis theirs) define attention as *"the set of evolved brain processes that leads to adaptive and effective behavioral selection,"* and, similarly, Wu (2024, 3) defines attention as "the subject mentally selecting a target to guide behavior." So, we can inquire as to what processes explain why one target rather than another in the environment is attended to (i.e., selected to guide behavior).[14]

---

[13] We'll go on to discuss how emotion affects our perception of a situation and our response to it separately in the sections that follow, but we're in agreement with Phan and Sripada's (2013, 376) claim that "[i]t is useful to divide the unfolding of an emotion into a perception/appraisal stage and response phase, though doing so does not imply that the stages are temporally non-overlapping or that the causal links between the stages are unidirectional."

[14] Both also argue that the reason why selective attention is beneficial is that it enhances goal-directed activity, and not that it's necessary because of limited cognitive resources. However, it's been a common assumption that since we have limited cognitive resources that we need a mechanism for filtering out most of the stimuli in the environment so that we limit it to a manageable amount of information to process, and that selective attention is this mechanism. This assumption shows up in some enactivist accounts, such as when Maiese (2014, 524) claims that emotions help us to "affectively frame" what's relevant in our environment, such that "[i]f subjects did not rely on affective framing, then they would be faced with a potentially endless array of possible cognitive and interpretive options, and this would make the task of adapting to their environments very difficult." While it is the case that we have cognitive limitations, this would merely place a constraint on attention in the sense of limiting how much we might attend to in our environment for guiding action, rather than showing that selective attention is necessary to cope with those limitations (Wu 2024, see also Krauzlis et al. 2024).

There are "bottom-up" processes for attention where a stimulus in our environment "grabs" our attention – a flash of light, a loud noise, and so on – because of its physical salience (and perhaps when it's unexpected). There are also "top-down" processes, such as those involved with active goal pursuit, where a particular target is selected because it is expected to yield the most relevant information for pursuing the goal.[15] For example, when driving one typically attends to the road and cars ahead because that provides the most relevant information to inform driving (when to slow down, change lanes, etc.), but sometimes one might instead select the GPS (maybe visually, maybe auditorily) to guide driving to know when next to turn. When driving in icy weather, it helps to try to feel the car's grip on the road to better guide decisions such as whether one is going too fast around a turn (whereas in dry weather that source of information tends not to be useful in guiding driving). So, one "tunes in" to whatever stream of information is taken to be the most helpful in guiding one's current goal-directed activity (e.g., arriving safely and efficiently at the intended destination), and where one's current goals explain what is selected as a target for guiding behavior.

Because of the connection discussed earlier between emotions and goals, and this connection between attention and goals, we can already start to see how emotions can play a functional role in our lives by drawing attention to aspects of our situation that are relevant to pursuing our goals+. The bodily feelings of emotion are registering something of significance in our environment, where this significance is relative to our cares and concerns. In other words, emotions play a mediating role between our concerns and the situations we encounter. Phan and Sripada (2013, 375) claim that "[e]motions attach salience to goal-relevant aspects of the environment and, once triggered, bias cognition and action in characteristic ways that have proven to be adaptive across evolutionary time." Features of our environment can become salient to us because they could potentially support or thwart our goals+. As a sensitivity to our environment which doesn't require conscious attention, the spontaneity of emotional

---

So, the "filtering" or "framing" that's associated with attention is a side effect of focusing on certain information to enhance goal pursuit, rather than a means to prevent sensory overload (Krauzlis et al. 2014, 458).

[15] While it is convenient to discuss "top-down" and "bottom-up" causes of selective attention, the underlying neurological processes may be the same (Krauzlis et al. 2024, 4). Also, as Wu (2011) noted, the "utility of having a capacity that renders an object salient to us despite our being involved in other activities is that it can serve our goals by forcing us to act on the relevant object." Thus, both forms of attention can be understood in terms of selection for action, and as such both are goal-driven processes. Top-down attention is guided by current goal pursuit (automatically or deliberatively), whereas bottom-up attention is guiding us to stimuli that might be relevant in promoting or threatening the current goal or other important goals.

responses likely provides a survival advantage in reacting quickly to emergency situations.[16]

So, emotions guide attention by boosting the expected relevance of specific stimuli (to our goals+) such that you're more likely to select those stimuli to guide your actions.[17] For example, the fear induced by the sight of a snake is an emotional response that's signaling that the presence of a nearby snake is highly relevant for how you ought to act now (i.e., avoid). Or, if you're a snake hunter, then the sight of the snake is likely to result instead in a feeling of joy, and this positive valence is also a signal that the presence of the snake ought to guide your actions because it will enhance your goals (i.e., approach). It's worth emphasizing here that it's our goals+ that are the basis for assigning those emotional tags to stimuli, and this helps to reinforce the point that our emotional responses are a pathway to gaining insight into the goals+ that are directing what we attend to in guiding our actions (which is especially relevant for goals that we have that aren't fully transparent to us).

3.4 Emotions Preparing Us for Action

Emotional responses draw our attention toward stimuli that are potentially relevant to acting upon in order to further our goals+ and they also involve some initial preparation for responding to those stimuli (Critchley & Nagai 2012). Since that preparation involves bodily changes, we will argue that this helps to explain why attending to the body is central to the acquisition of emotional self-knowledge and therefore is also linked to greater self-knowledge of our goals+, and thus better mental health and well-being outcomes.

---

[16] How do emotions attach salience to goal-relevant stimuli, such that it guides our attention? Taylor and Fragopanagos (2005), in a discussion of the neuroscience behind how emotional appraisals guide our attention, describe the role of processes for emotionally "tagging" stimuli with positive or negative valence, where the effect of such tagging is to boost the relevance of that stimuli when selecting a target for guiding action (i.e., guiding attention toward that stimuli). They provide some helpful examples of this: "the emotional tag of fear can be attached to a threatening stimulus in so far as the latter can potentially impede the goal of survival. Another example is the emotional tag of happiness that can be assigned to any stimulus that advances the goal of well-being. In a similar fashion numerous emotional tags can be given to stimuli that promote or hinder the attainment of goals ranging from basic individual survival goals to more complex social interaction goals" (Taylor and Fragopanagos 2005, 354).

[17] A nonconscious monitoring of our environment is crucial to remain adaptive to changing situations, and emotional responses play a key role in this monitoring. Though, since emotional responses involve a pre-reflective appraisal, we may not fully appreciate how much emotion helps to guide us in day-to-day functioning (such as by guiding our attention). It may be that we tend to underestimate the role of emotion in navigating our environment, and that we pay attention to emotions only when they misfire. In which case, we might come to associate these capacities with their potential for error, and then we might be inclined to focus on minimizing the impact of emotions and to devalue their contribution to making judgments.

We think it will be helpful to supplement enactive theories of emotion with further research from affective neuroscience to ground embodied appraisals in core affect and, thus, in interoceptive predictions. In this way, we offer a robust, neurobiological understanding of how the body makes "judgments" or appraisals in the form of interoceptive predictions. Specifically, we draw on core affect to specify the informational nature of embodied appraisals and to spell out how it is that the body itself could play this informational role. After all, it has long been assumed that cognition is informational and representational while the body is mechanical. On our view, this long-standing assumption is false. This move also helps us to see that the cares and concerns that embodied appraisals reveal are values and priorities as registered by our bodies, not at the level of the person, but at the level of the organism.

Our suggestion is that embodied appraisals ought to be identified with core affect, which is itself constituted by interoceptive predictions. Interoceptive predictions are states of the autonomic nervous system that respond to environmental and internal stimuli with immediate physiological adjustments, for example, heart rate, respiration, blood pressure, bodily temperature, digestion, and perspiration (as we explained earlier: Craig 2003; Critchley & Garfinkel 2017; Khalsa et al. 2018). For our purposes, it is critical to notice that in addition to their role in maintaining physiological homeostasis, it is widely accepted that interoceptive states constitute a core component of emotion and mood (Feldman-Barrett 2017; Russell 2003). This core component of emotion is called "core affect" and refers to the basic bodily feelings or sensations that are characteristic of emotional experiences. It has further been shown using neuroimaging by Zaki et al. (2012, 497) that "bodily feelings and emotional experience share overlapping information processing mechanisms." To be clear, our claim is that emotions involve basic bodily feelings that are produced by interoceptive mechanisms and their immediate neurobiological expressions.

This helps to explain why affect feels a certain way – because at least some bodily changes create subjective changes for the agent – that is, when your heart races and your breath becomes shallow, it feels a certain way to you. Additionally, interoceptive predictions also help account for the motivational aspect of affect because, first and foremost, interoceptive predictions prepare the body for action (fight, flight, freeze, engage, avoid, etc.). One way of thinking of this kind of prediction is as a pushmi-pullyu representation (Millikan 1995). That is, the prediction not only represents what is expected but in representing the expectation it alters the neural, biological, chemical, psychological, and behavioral organization of the organism in preparation for action (though this preparedness by itself doesn't necessitate a specific action in response, so talk of emotions having an "action tendency" should be understood in more general terms like approach or avoidance).

This view is especially potent if we think of interoceptive mechanisms, including those involved in core affect, as having the basic function of predicting the expected energy needs of an organism. As Lisa Feldman-Barrett (2017, 69) explains:

> your brain must constantly predict your body's energy needs, like a budget for your body. Just as a company has a finance department that tracks deposits and withdrawals and moves money between accounts, so its overall budget stays in balance, your brain has circuitry that is largely responsible for your body budget. That circuitry is within your interoceptive network. Your body-budgeting regions make predictions to estimate the resources to keep you alive and flourishing, using your past experience as a guide.

In this way, while core affect is somewhat basic – certainly not conceptual or propositional – it still implements an informational function. That is, core affect, grounded in interoceptive predictions, conveys contextually relevant embodied information about the type and amount of energy that will be needed by an organism to cope with its environment. This is done by registering information on two dimensions: valence and arousal (Barrett 2017; Russell 2003). The first dimension is felt as pleasant or unpleasant sensations, and the second produces feelings of calmness or jitteriness, activation or deactivation.[18] Accordingly, the first dimension evaluates what kind of situation one is dealing with, for example, positive or negative while the arousal component anticipates the requisite intensity of action. All these predictions happen at the bodily level, the level of the nervous system. But what they reveal to us is the way the body evaluates our environment, the situations we face, the events, people, and objects. These predictions reveal expectations of the body, given its current state and future needs – is this food going to be delicious? Is this mate going to be reliable? Is this book going to be boring?

It is also worth mentioning that interoceptive predictions are not fixed biologically but adjust in response to previous experience, perhaps like Bayesian priors. In this way, interoceptive predictions use past experiences to determine future expectations. If a situation was dangerous in the past, then the interceptive system should predict that it will be dangerous in the future: hence unpleasant valence and some degree of intensity or arousal. Another way of saying this is that the interoceptive prediction evaluates the situation as dangerous. Or, the situation is appraised, in a bodily way, as dangerous. If a person has

---

[18] So, while we don't have direct access to the interoceptive predictions, we do indirectly via the experience of valence and arousal associated with core affect.

been reliable and friendly in the past, then the interoceptive system will register predictions in terms of positive valence and mild arousal – because the energy needed to cope with this interaction is low, based on past interactions. The interoceptive prediction is of a friendly interaction with this person. Or, the appraisal of this person, in a bodily way, is that of friendliness.

To be clear, then, the research supports a view in which the predictions of interoceptive mechanisms which constitute core affect are encoded directly into neurophysiological processes. These predictions, we think, are an empirically informed way of spelling out embodied appraisal. If we think of embodied appraisals as identical to core affect and think of core affect as constituted by interoceptive predictions, then we have a clear explanation of how it is that the body can play the informational role that embodied appraisal theorists need it to play. It also helps us to make clear why it is that attending to the body is a way of accessing affective self-knowledge – because affective states are at their very core bodily – and so attending to the information provided by bodily experience gives us a window into our underlying emotional processes and, thus, to the values, cares, concerns, and priorities of our informational, biological body.

4 Emotions and Self-Knowledge

What are some initial implications of the connection we've been arguing for between emotions and goals+ for self-knowledge? First, we think the connection between emotions and goals supports a strong claim that awareness of our emotions, and affective reactions more generally, give us self-knowledge directly. To feel is already to know. However, that claim must be tempered by the fact that what we are justified in believing initially might be fairly limited in content[19] – to know merely that something about our current situation potentially promotes or obstructs one's goals+. For example, recognizing that you're in a bad mood is to already know that something is out of alignment, and that should give you a reason to figure out what's going on in more detail in order to take effective action in response. But increasing our knowledge about the nature of the affordance or conflict (i.e., which of our goals are at stake, in what way are they potentially affected by the situation, etc.), along with knowing how to appropriately respond to the situation, will involve more complex processes (inference, skill, etc.) as we'll discuss in the sections that follow. Furthermore, it's worth emphasizing the related implication which is that insofar as any emotional reaction gives us some degree of knowledge,

---

[19] Though as we'll go on to argue, emotional skills could enable us to have greater knowledge that's apprehended immediately.

we have epistemic and practical reasons to pay attention to emotion rather than to dismiss it as irrelevant or irrational.

Second, we think that part of the reason why acquiring greater self-knowledge of our emotional states can be a means by which we can acquire further self-knowledge about our goals+ is because our goals+ are not always transparent to us, and so might helpfully be revealed to us in how we feel. After all, if our goals, values, interests, cares, and concerns were always fully transparent to us, then our emotional states wouldn't provide us information about ourselves that we didn't already know. But, for example, you might not realize that someone is fulfilling an important need in your life until they're no longer there and you feel that loss. On this note, Cholbi (2019) has an insightful discussion of grief as a motivator for acquiring self-knowledge. He notes that in "undergoing joy, anxiety, anger, etc., as stages in a grief process, we are afforded an opportunity to catalog or take stock of the fundamental cares or concerns around which we organize our lives" (Cholbi 2019, 501). So, insofar as we dismiss or ignore our emotional reactions, we lose out on opportunities to access some further knowledge about ourselves. Hence, in the sections that follow, we'll draw out some ways in which self-knowledge of our bodily and emotional states can provide us with further types of self-knowledge.

4.1 From Bodily Self-Knowledge to Emotional Self-Knowledge

So far, we've provided a framework for understanding why there's a connection between our bodily states and our emotional experiences (and why emotional experiences reveal our goals+). Our view is thus similar to Goldie's (2002, 237) claim that "certain bodily feelings can and do provide a prima facie reason for one's believing that one is experiencing an emotion of a certain type." Thus, knowledge of the former should yield knowledge of the latter – but there's still a question of how. So, we'll next provide some examples of ways in which people attend to their bodily experiences and then explain how it is that this bodily self-knowledge can provide us with further emotional self-knowledge, and thus further self-knowledge of our goals+ (though we take this to be just the start of a robust account of these connections).

One example of bodily self-knowledge yielding insight into emotional self-knowledge comes from Füstös et al.'s (2012) studies on interoceptive awareness in relation to emotion regulation. They speculated that since "emotion regulation requires the awareness of one's emotional and bodily state, it can be followed that a high awareness of interoceptive signals might facilitate emotion regulation by supporting the detection of early bodily reactions in response to emotional stimuli" (2012, 912). In other words, emotion regulation requires being aware of your emotional state, and since bodily changes will accompany an emotional response, the sooner you're aware of those bodily changes (i.e., interoceptive signals) taking place, the more informed you will be about your current emotional state. Given this, Füstös et al. did a study on the relationship between interoceptive awareness (i.e., interoceptive self-knowledge) and emotional reappraisal strategies, as the latter are well-documented to be successful strategies for emotion regulation. Reappraisal strategies seek to change the initial appraisal of a situation that gave rise to an emotional response, typically by reinterpreting the situation as less negative such that it no longer feels as distressing (since the emotional response is based on how the situation is appraised). For example, one could change an initial appraisal of critical comments on a paper from indications of failure to suggestions for improvement. Importantly, as Gross and John (2003, 349) point out in their studies on emotion regulation, "[r]eappraisal is an antecedent-focused strategy: it occurs early, and intervenes before the emotion response tendencies have been fully generated." This implies that this strategy can be used early in the unfolding of an emotional response to downregulate negative affect (and where the effectiveness of the strategy is partly due to it being an early intervention which effects the subsequent unfolding of the emotional response).[20]

Füstös et al. measured interoceptive awareness (IA) by measuring how accurately individuals could detect the rate of their heartbeats internally, without relying on checking for their pulse (and different tasks can measure respiratory, gastric, or other forms of IA). They used electrophysiological measures to document that those with higher IA showed a greater down-regulation of negative affect when using emotional reappraisal strategies. They claimed that the "findings suggest that the more aware a person is of ongoing bodily processes, the more successful this person's emotion regulation in response to negative affect will be" (Füstös et al. 2012, 914–915). This makes sense if attending to one's ongoing bodily processes is providing information that's relevant to guiding the task of emotion regulation, and that would imply that interoceptive awareness is providing insight into one's emotional experiences.

Relatedly, Füstös et al. reference work done by Herbert et al. (2007) that can help us understand more precisely the connection between interoceptive awareness and self-regulation. Herbert et al. studied IA in the context of exercise and physical effort, and demonstrated that those with higher IA of their cardiac

---

[20] While emotions are often viewed as something in need of regulation when they're excessive, it's often the cognitive element of the appraisal that's the problem, hence the success of cognitive reappraisal strategies. But in that sense, it's unfair to view the problem as stemming from emotion rather than cognition as the emotional response is based on a faulty cognitive input (and given that emotion and cognition are interwoven).

system were better able to guide their levels of exertion due to the greater accuracy in the perception of their levels of fatigue. By contrast, those with lower IA had less accurate views of their fatigue levels, which they were prone to underestimating, and consequently were overexerting themselves and making themselves more vulnerable to physical strain. Füstös et al. (2012, 915) see their experiments as building on this, and they "suggest that interoceptive sensitivity for bodily changes in one physiological system (such as the cardiac system) relevantly mediates emotion regulation in situations evoking physiological activity in these bodily systems." So, because emotional processes involve changes in core affect (e.g., changes in specific physiological systems), then greater interoceptive awareness of those systems will enable faster (and more accurate) recognition of when changes are occurring there because of an emotional response. This should aid in acquiring better self-knowledge of one's emotional states, via emotion differentiation, since emotions can differ in their associated physiological changes. Also, since these physiological changes occur at the outset of emotional processes, being aware of those changes as they unfold enables the use of early emotion regulation strategies like reappraisal (Price & Hooven 2018).

Given the benefits of greater IA, we next inquire into some methods for improving IA, and mindfulness training has proven effective in this regard. Price and Hooven (2018) describe a particular form of "Mindful awareness in body-oriented therapy" (MABT) that aims at developing greater IA. The training begins by practicing the identification of bodily sensations, such as by "(a) attending to and feeling the sensation and flow of exhaled breath through the body, (b) using intention to feel the softening of areas of muscular tension, and (c) bringing attention to a specific area of internal body (e.g., inside chest, shoulder girdle, abdomen, etc.)" (Price & Hooven 2018, 6). This training is designed to direct one's attention to inner bodily sensations to become aware of what information is present in those locations (e.g., tension), and then that can be coupled with learning about the significance of that information (e.g., stress), such that it can eventually be used to guide action (e.g., techniques to reduce the stress before it builds up too much).

Along with learning to identify important bodily sensations, MABT also involves the practice of naming these sensations to be able to describe them with some precision. Price and Hooven (2018, 5) explain the reasoning behind this, as:

> the ability to identify and describe sensation is fundamental for interoceptive awareness as it provides a pathway for relating or associating to the body, and thus facilitates perceived linkages between experiences of sensation (i.e.,

links between physical and emotional awareness, for example increased muscular tension and anger) and linkages between sensation and environmental triggers.

So, going back to the framework of emotions as embodied appraisals, having greater bodily self-knowledge enables one to gain further knowledge about their emotional states because they're gaining information about: (1) the links between bodily changes as preparedness for action and aspects of the emotional processes that are causing them (i.e., valence and arousal of the appraisal, approach or avoidance tendencies); and (2) the links between the bodily changes and what stimuli in their environment (both internal and external) might have triggered the emotional process (i.e., what the appraisal was about). Furthermore, an earlier detection of bodily changes would facilitate accuracy with respect to knowing what triggered the emotional process, as the more time passes before one recognizes their emotional state the harder it can be to trace what originally triggered that state (i.e., a greater chance of misattribution). This emotional self-knowledge can then facilitate the use of a variety of emotion regulation strategies as well (especially reappraisal strategies that are effective when used early in the unfolding of an emotional response).

4.2 From Bodily Self-Knowledge to Goals+ Self-Knowledge

Bodily self-knowledge can also provide insight into our goals, values, interests, cares, and concerns more directly. An example of how better attending to one's bodily states can also further self-knowledge about one's goals+ can be seen in stories told by former restaurant employees in the wake of the COVID-19 pandemic when they considered going back to their previous jobs. During this time, many people who lost jobs working in the restaurant industry during COVID-19 lockdowns were not willing to go back to them when the restaurants reopened, leading to a large shortage in employees across the country. For some, it ended up being an opportunity to realize the toll that working sixty or more hours a week for minimal pay was taking on them, with them being on their feet all day and working in sweltering kitchens or dealing with abusive customers. One former restaurant employee noted that he was initially considering taking another restaurant job as soon as one opened:

> And then, the thing that happened for me is that, I started to notice how well rested I was. The bags that were under my eyes forever – for years – went away. My feet stopped hurting, and I never had really thought about how much my feet hurt all the time, but they did. My back stopped hurting. . . . And so I started thinking like, well, why am I really doing this? Is this really

serving me, or is it just serving whoever my employer is? And the easy answer to that question is, it isn't serving me.[21]

Importantly, it wasn't until this person started attending to the felt differences in his body that he started questioning what was of value to him, and what kind of job could be more fulfilling to him. It's of course unfortunate that it took something as dramatic as losing one's job during a pandemic to provide an opportunity to experience life differently, but for the millions of people working over forty hours a week to survive there would have been few opportunities to do so otherwise.

People in such stressful situations can become somewhat numb to their pain, preventing either an awareness of the pain or paying attention to the significance of it. Price and Hooven (2018, 3) describe the implication of this kind of "hypo" sensitivity to bodily sensation, which is that a "buffered responsivity is less informed and engaged, and therefore less likely to respond when responding is called for. Hence, the excessive and/or unrelenting demands from a difficult environment can get 'under the skin' and change a person's physiological response to stress." The employee *on some level* knew that his feet hurt all the time, but it didn't prompt him to question what he was doing until he could experience not hurting for an extended period of time – that felt difference was crucial as feedback for changing how he was attending to what his body was signaling to him. Whereas before he might have attended to that pain in terms of taking actions to temporarily relieve that pain (e.g., elevating or icing his feet), now this pain was taking on new significance (i.e., it was being seen as relevant to acting on setting broader goals+), and so guiding him to reflect on and reevaluate his career and how he wanted his life to go.[22] The point that we want to emphasize here is that affective and bodily experiences constitute a key ground for our coming to know about our own cares and concerns. It is not that these kinds of experiences are just another mental state for our self-knowledge to target. Rather, they form a critical foundation for our coming to learn about the things that matter to us most.

4.3 From Emotional Self-Knowledge to Goals+ Self-Knowledge

We maintain that the way in which we as organisms experience the world provides us with information that is vital to our well-being because it allows

---

[21] Stories From the Great American Labor Shortage, Tuesday, August 3, 2021, www.nytimes.com/2021/08/03/podcasts/the-daily/coronavirus-hiring-job-vacancies-hospitality-industry.html?showTranscript=1.

[22] This recognition of suffering might also prompt reflection on the broader economic and political structures that cause or contribute to this suffering, and so might also motivate promoting social change. For the connection between bodily suffering and social change, see Leeb (2018a).

us to identify values, cares, and concerns in a way that is grounded in our own experience and not only in general principles, cultural norms, or less than ideal histories. This kind of emotional knowledge – knowledge of how we feel in response to various situations, people and events – is indispensable for knowing what we care about. What we then do with that knowledge – whether we use it to guide decisions, actions, relationships, and plans or reject it and attempt to gain clarity concerning where it comes from and what might be done to intervene on it, regulate it, or align it with one's *all things considered* judgment – is an opportunity that arises on the back of that knowledge.

So, in addition to some of the benefits of bodily and affective self-knowledge for emotion regulation and thus better mental health outcomes, we think another piece in the puzzle of why this self-knowledge leads to better well-being outcomes stems from how an awareness of our own emotional experiences provides us with the opportunity to also use that self-knowledge for decision-making, goal setting, and action planning. That is, emotional self-knowledge plays an important instrumental role in guiding some of our most core activities as people.[23] Furthermore, we contend that this kind of self-knowledge of our goals+ is not necessarily given (e.g., found out through simple introspection), and that our affective-bodily reactions provide valuable insight into whether activities we're engaged in are fulfilling or meaningful.

We start with a fictional example of making a difficult choice about which career to pursue to illustrate what we have in mind in terms of making impactful decisions, which suggests that being in better contact with our affective and bodily states is a promising route for acquiring self-knowledge and making better decisions. We then review the evidence from self-regulation theory in psychology that suggests that emotional self-knowledge does aid in this kind of goal setting and pursuit.

4.3.1 An Example: What Career Should Alan Pursue?

Alan has just finished his PhD in psychology and is deciding between pursuing an academic job which would involve research, publishing, and teaching and could provide him with a respected career path in line with many of the expectations of his fellow grad students and professors, but which will commit

---

[23] A straightforward case can be made that self-knowledge of our goals+ can be instrumentally valuable for our pursuits, which Cassam (2014, 212) refers to as a "low road" explanation of the value of self-knowledge (and it's the road he favors). While it might turn out that there are also "high road" explanations that claim that self-knowledge is intrinsically valuable (beyond whatever instrumental value it has for our lives), for our own purposes we take our account to be sufficiently motivated by the instrumental value of self-knowledge of our goals+. If this self-knowledge also turns out to be of intrinsic value, so much the better!

him to a brutal job search, a life of grant applications, conference travel, and an all but guaranteed change in geographical location. Alan has also considered pursuing a clinical career in psychology, working with patients in a local inpatient setting where he has conducted a lot of the research for his dissertation. This work would involve intense emotional labor, working intimately with patients in substance abuse recovery and would have limited travel and no change of location. Both careers will make Alan about the same amount of money. How should Alan decide what he should do after he has collected all the facts about the two career paths?

Should Alan do *more* research to see if most people who move to locations for work are happier than those that don't? Should Alan research if academics are happier than psychotherapists? Should he try to find out if meeting the expectations of esteemed colleagues makes for a good life? Alan could do all of these things, but he also needs to see how this information connects up to his values, preferences, interests, and so on (e.g., a job where you'll mostly be working alone will be valued differently depending on how much you like to be surrounded by other people). But it may be that what Alan is struggling with just is his own assessment of what's important *to him* and what brings vitality into *his life*. In which case, what Alan needs to do is to figure out what he likes, enjoys, feels energized by, is most proud of, and so on. Alan needs to learn what he values, what he prioritizes, and what's important to him.

But how can he do this? That is, how does one figure out what is satisfying to oneself? Shouldn't one consult one's own experiential and affective reactions? After all, no amount of deliberation about writing can ultimately tell Alan if he *likes* writing papers. Because to figure this out, he needs to do more than think about writing papers, he needs to pay attention to how it feels for him to write. No amount of deliberating can ultimately tell Alan if he *enjoys* doing emotional work. He has to notice what he feels – energized or depleted?

The point is that Alan can turn toward his own emotions, investigate and examine them, and become familiar with their subjective qualities, their valence, and intensity. That is, Alan can develop the capacity to know how various situations, events, people, and circumstances make him feel *in his body*, and then use that information as a guide to his values, cares, and concerns. Further, the question for Alan isn't, primarily, is writing valuable, *full stop*? The question is: is writing valuable *for me?* It is this aspect of value, first and foremost, that emotions give us epistemic access to, since emotions are appraisals based on our goals+, and that we must turn toward to more fully know ourselves. In some ways, these assertions seem so obvious and yet, in others, we can't help but notice that these facts are both underappreciated and undertheorized.

4.4 The Value of Emotional Self-Knowledge for Setting Goals

In understanding how self-knowledge is relevant to making these kinds of important life choices, we can helpfully draw on theories of self-regulation in psychology that are meant to explain how organisms are motivated to regulate their behavior according to goals. When it comes to theories of human self-regulation, a goal is a desired state of affairs which one puts effort into achieving. The goal provides motivation to take actions to achieve it, and this involves monitoring our progress toward the goal (or adherence to an enduring standard) and responding to feedback about whether our actions are helping or hindering us in striving toward the goal.[24]

There are two important criteria to consider with goal setting, which are the desirability and the feasibility of the goal. Desirability is a matter of how valued the attainment of the goal is to the person. Feasibility is a matter of considering how likely it is that one can accomplish a goal. This involves assessing the difficulty of the goal, how much effort or what amount of resources one would have to put into achieving the goal, and whether one has the necessary capacities to succeed (which are often referred to as self-efficacy beliefs).[25] The feasibility of a goal can be determined by deliberating about the challenges involved with achieving the goal and how well one is positioned to overcome those challenges. Building on this, we hope to show that having self-knowledge of goals+ is valuable for setting and revising goals, like with the example of choosing a career, and that emotions help to provide this relevant self-knowledge.

Importantly, what gets overlooked in discussions of goal setting is the fact that the desirability of a goal is not something that can be determined using the strategies of instrumental rationality. After all, what we are trying to figure out here is not which means to use but what our ends should be.[26] Some of our

---

[24] There's also an important distinction between the processes involved with setting goals versus processes relevant in striving for goals. In the latter, we have a goal that we are going to put effort into achieving and, in some sense, the goal is "fixed" (at least temporarily), and so the focus is on how best to achieve it. Whereas with goal setting, the question is whether to adopt a new goal or to revise or reject an existing goal.

[25] A part of determining feasibility will likely draw on strategies associated with goal striving, in the sense that you might need to think about how you would strive to accomplish a goal, to determine how easy or difficult it may be to accomplish.

[26] Aristotle seemed to have recognized this distinction between goal setting and goal striving, and the different processes involved, when he claimed that "We deliberate not about ends, but about means. For a doctor does not deliberate whether he shall heal, nor an orator whether he shall convince, nor a statesman whether he shall produce law and order, nor does anyone else deliberate about his end" (NE 1112b12-20). In other words, the doctor already has a set goal of healing. If we understand "deliberate" as narrowly referring to instrumental reasoning regarding how we effectively strive for a goal, then the doctor can deliberate about how best to heal a patient but would not be using that type of instrumental reasoning to set goals. Different processes and skills need to be involved to help us figure out how to set goals (Moss 2011). But, if

values may be set through good reasons and arguments, for example (hopefully), moral and political values. But often, information about desirability comes in the form of bodily affective feedback because reason and argument alone are simply ill-suited for determining desirability in all cases. This relationship between goals and emotional feedback can be seen in studies of the use of goal-imagery. Goal-imagery refers to vividly imagining the striving and achievement of a goal and then seeing how that makes one feel. Schultheiss and Brunstein (1999, 6) proposed that

> engaging in goal imagery helps a person realize what it would mean to strive for a specific goal by experiencing how emotionally satisfying its pursuit and attainment would be for him or her. This experience, in turn, should help the person decide whether to commit himself or herself to the goal or not, depending on whether or not he or she was emotionally aroused by the goal imagery.

Their studies provided evidence that those who engaged in goal-imagery and experienced positive affective arousal as a result were more committed to achieving the goal. What's important to note is that it wasn't necessarily transparent to those in the studies whether the pursuit of the goal would be meaningful or fulfilling, and that their emotional reaction to the use of goal-imagery was providing feedback that could help them to figure out how desirable it might be to achieve the goal.

While we often choose to adopt goals, it's also the case that goals can be something we are mostly unaware of, as growing up with a specific biological and cultural background can impart goals that are "inherited" due to a shared cultural or social understanding (social norms, rules of games, standards of good artistic performance, etc.). These can sometimes be the result of coercive pressures or oppression and, as such, not so "freely" chosen (as we'll discuss further with cases of "outlaw" emotions). Tiberius and DeYoung (2022, 170), in their goal-fulfillment account of well-being, discuss how goals that we are unaware of can still guide our actions, and helpfully draw attention to the role of feelings and emotion in becoming more aware of them, explaining that:

> goals can be unconscious, hence unable to be articulated in language, and they may be relatively vague and only generally specified. Like conscious goals, unconscious and vague goals are taken to be actually represented in the brain and to have important potential consequences for well-being. The fact that a goal state is hidden from consciousness does not mean it has no effects,

---

we understand "deliberate" more broadly to include how we sometimes weigh competing goals to decide which to pursue, then in this sense we do deliberate about ends (Kolnai 1978). Though that broader kind of deliberation in setting and revising goals will still differ from the kind of means-end reasoning used in goal striving.

as such goals can nonetheless influence behavior, decisions, and emotional reactions (Latham et al. 2017; Schultheiss and Strasser 2012; Tiberius & DeYoung 2022). This is one of the reasons that paying attention to our feelings (such as unexplained bad feelings or "negative mystery moods"; Chartrand et al. 2010) is a good strategy for happiness.... Attending to feelings that do not have immediately obvious causes can help us to discover unconscious goals, thereby facilitating their integration with conscious goals.[27]

So, by the time we are cognitively mature enough to reflect on what goals we might want to choose for ourselves, we have already internalized various goals that to some extent guide our day-to-day behavior. With respect to goal setting, while sometimes we are considering whether to adopt a new goal, there are also potential revisions to make regarding any one of our existing "inherited" goals – such as whether to reevaluate, revise, or reject the goal. Given that conceptions of goals and motives to adopt them come to us through our cultural and social environment, this revaluation process is likely to be carried out in discussion and reflection with others.

4.5 Conflicts and the Case of Outlaw Emotions

But what about cases in which our emotional reactions seem to clash with our deliberative judgments, especially when those judgments are reinforced by one's cultural and social environment? Should we still trust that we're getting reliable information from our emotional reactions in such cases?

We don't think there will be a one-size-fits-all answer to such questions. However, we do think it's important to emphasize that such questions shouldn't necessarily be resolved always in favor of our reflective judgments over our emotional reactions when we're internally conflicted (which we take to be a common assumption), and we'll use cases of "outlaw" emotions under conditions of oppression to illustrate this point. Furthermore, even when it's fitting to think there is something mistaken about our emotional reactions and there's no need to revise our reflective judgments, say in cases of implicit bias, it's still important to attend to these reactions (rather than ignore them) as they still provide knowledge about ourselves that can be relevant for further action (e.g., taking steps to counter sources of an implicit bias).

In Silva's (2021) discussion of outlaw emotions, she draws on an example from Marilyn Friedman (1986, 31), which will be helpful to discuss at length:

---

[27] They also note that on their account, since well-being is increased by having one's goals fulfilled, one thing that will interfere with well-being are conflicts between one's goals (either conscious or unconscious). Thus, becoming more aware of unconscious goals, by attending to our affective and emotional responses, can help us uncover such potential goal conflicts.

Emotional Self-Knowledge 31

Discontent Housewife:
A woman who has been taught that a 'woman's place is in the home' may be driven to question this maxim precisely in light of her persistent dissatisfactions and repeated urges to flee from the responsibilities and limitations which structure her domestic life ... if her highest principles themselves also include notions of 'appropriate' sex roles, duties to others and the importance of self-sacrifice as an ideal of femininity, then there is not much available among her highest principles to afford an independent standpoint for assessing the maxim about woman's place. Her frustration, grief, and depression, and the motivations to change her life which spring from these sources, may be her only reliable guides.

As we understand such a case, the housewife is experiencing a variety of negative emotions, and so there's clearly a disconnect between her domestic activities and her goals, values, interests, cares, and concerns. Since there's no indication that these emotions spring from a failure to succeed in her role or duties, they instead imply that her activities are failing to provide the satisfaction she might otherwise be expected to experience in living up to the "ideal of femininity." So, the emotions she experiences provide her with relevant self-knowledge about her goals+ – namely that they don't currently match up with her assigned sex roles and duties. She may have thought she endorsed the sex roles, but clearly part of her strongly rejects them, and she likely has goals+ that are actively thwarted by her daily activities (and hence the "persistent dissatisfactions and repeated urges to flee").

While this perspective on the case doesn't dictate a particular way of resolving the conflict, Friedman notes that at the very least it can motivate some reflection on what might have otherwise been taken for granted – that a 'woman's place is in the home.' Silva (2021, 668) describes this as the "Motivational View" about the epistemic role of emotions, and Jones (2003, 186) highlights that:

Our efforts to make sense of outlaw emotions can provide a starting point for the critical re-examination of even quite central evaluative assumptions. Thus, emotions can function as recalcitrant data that force a change in our evaluative assumptions.

Furthermore, the negative affect that the discontented housewife experiences will continue until she finds a way to resolve the conflict (after all, that's the function of negative affect – to motivate taking action that's relevant to one's goals+). So, it will certainly not help for her to treat her emotional responses as irrational or irrelevant – they are quite reliable in indicating a conflict, and, as such, her retreating from or dismissing them will not help her to solve this conflict.

Silva (2021, 664) provides a helpful characterization of outlaw emotions that brings out several key points worth considering in further detail, as she claims that:

> Outlaw emotions are emotions that stand in tension with a large set of an agent's beliefs. They are recalcitrant emotions, as they conflict with the agent's evaluative judgements, but they are not merely recalcitrant. In typical cases of recalcitrant emotion, such as fear of a dog that one believes is not dangerous, there need be only one belief that the emotion conflicts with. In outlaw emotion cases, although there is typically a belief with which the emotion conflicts, making the emotion recalcitrant, the emotion also stands in tension with a large set of further beliefs, often clashing with an agent's wider belief system.

The first key point is that outlaw emotions are a subset of recalcitrant emotions (D'Arms and Jacobson 2003; Brady 2009; Majeed 2022), and, as we'll later argue, that recalcitrance by itself is significant for self-knowledge.[28] Second, while outlaw emotions are typically discussed in the context of a wider belief system that has been shaped by oppressive ideologies, as Silva notes (2021, 665–666), this definition is broad enough to include tensions that arise for other reasons. For example, one might experience emotional responses that conflict with one's wider belief system but where that wider belief system includes egalitarian ideals. This could include conflicting emotional responses that stem from implicit bias (where oppression might be responsible for forming the bias but not the wider belief system). For example, one might think they're dedicated to values of justice, but fail to display appropriate emotional reactions to injustice when it happens to members of an out-group. Or, as a non-ideological example, one might identify themselves as a classical music lover but find at some point that they start feeling restless when attending classical music concerts. Or you might like to think of yourself as being unconcerned with how others view you yet nonetheless experience emotions of embarrassment or humiliation in front of others which conflict with that self-conception. Hence, as mentioned in the discussion of the "discontent housewife," there isn't necessarily one right way to resolve conflicts stemming from outlaw emotions.

Third, a point which Silva doesn't raise is that since emotions are appraisals relative to our goals+, then a conflict could stem from a clash of goals as well as beliefs. Silva (2021, 669) does discuss the "Justificatory View" of the epistemic role of emotions in providing not just a motivation for inquiry but also a defeasible justification for beliefs. But it's common in discussions of outlaw

---

[28] There's a significant literature on recalcitrant emotions and rationality, but our interest here is what recalcitrant emotions imply for self-knowledge.

emotions to put the focus narrowly on the justification for beliefs connected to the emotional responses as specifically external appraisals (e.g., the beliefs in an oppressive ideology), while leaving out how those emotional responses might justify beliefs connected to internal appraisals. For example, it's not just that the negative emotions the discontented housewife feels are calling into question the sexist ideology, it's importantly the case that they're doing so in virtue of those beliefs requiring her to do things that are undermining other goals+ that she has. As the case is described, it's not merely that she fulfills her domestic duties but doesn't get great joy out of it, but rather that she feels "frustration, grief, and depression" instead. Those emotional responses would be explained by her having current goals+ that conflict with the dominant sexist ideology. That's the relevant self-knowledge that can be gained by attending to one's emotional responses, but this point about self-knowledge is frequently left out of the picture in discussions of outlaw emotions in general.

But is that self-knowledge of one's current goals+ of any benefit to the discontented housewife? Possibly, as the situation might not be as dire as Silva fears, for she (2021, 677) claims that oppressed people in these situations:

> likely lack access to the reasons for their emotions. Reflection is likely to favour the conflicting oppressive proposition given that they inhabit, and have internalized, oppressive ideology. It is therefore unlikely that agents in outlaw emotion cases are in a position to reflectively undermine their oppressive beliefs.

If "reasons for their emotions" reads in reference to only the sexist ideology, then perhaps people often lack access to fitting critiques of that ideology, and so reflection is unlikely to undermine belief in the ideology. But if "reasons for their emotions" reads in reference to their own goals+, then a recognition that one has valued goals that conflict with the ideology (independence, self-care, etc.) might give one further reasons to consider in questioning that ideology.

Though it's also possible in these situations that one is experiencing conflicts between their goals – some of them adopted because of oppressive ideology and other goals adopted independently of that. Jaggar (1989, 165) makes clear in her discussion of outlaw emotions that oppressive ideologies are likely to have influenced our goals+ as well, and she argues that:

> Within a hierarchical society, the norms and values that predominate tend to serve the interests of the dominant groups. Within a capitalist, white supremacist, and male-dominant society, the predominant values will tend to be those that serve the interests of rich white men. Consequently, we are all likely to develop an emotional constitution that is quite inappropriate for feminism. Whatever our color, we are likely to feel what Irving Thalberg has called

'visceral racism'; whatever our sexual orientation, we are likely to be homophobic; whatever our class, we are likely to be at least somewhat ambitious and competitive; whatever our sex, we are likely to feel contempt for women. Such emotional responses may be rooted in us so deeply that they are relatively impervious to intellectual argument and may recur even when we pay lip service to changed intellectual convictions.

Given this, it's to be expected that people will feel some positive emotions stemming from internalized oppressive goals (e.g., someone taking pride in fulfilling their stereotyped role). While these emotional responses would also be problematic, they won't by their nature be likely to motivate any change (since positive affect would instead reinforce similar behavior). However, Jagger (1989, 166) highlights that the occurrence of outlaw emotions is a sign that "the hegemony that our society exercises over people's emotional constitution is not total." A similar point is raised by Leeb (2018b), in her discussion of an embodied form of reflective judgment, that there is a "moment of the limit" in society's shaping of our feelings and thoughts, and that when individuals experience this moment they are in a position to challenge the dominant ideology. In such cases, it should also be expected that people will feel mixed emotional responses, with some responses stemming from oppressive goals and other responses stemming from valued personal goals that conflict with those oppressive goals. This again should be a cause of investigation into the sources of the conflict, and here Jaggar (1989, 170) helpfully points out the value of feminist and other critical social theories in providing us insights into society and how it's shaped our values and resulting emotional constitution.[29]

Overall, we don't intend to offer a recipe here for figuring out how to resolve conflicts generated by outlaw emotions, as others have pointed out the difficulties in doing so (Jaggar 1989, 168; Jones 2003, 197; Silva 2021, 688). But ignoring or dismissing one's emotional responses won't help. As Jaggar (1989, 169) perfectly sums up: "[a]ccepting the indispensability of appropriate emotions to knowledge means no more (and no less) than that discordant emotions should be attended to seriously and respectfully rather than condemned, ignored, discounted or suppressed." This is true even in the case of merely recalcitrant emotions, as in those cases there's still some part of your "system" that is still supplying a mistaken input into your emotional response, and you may have work to do to fix that (therapy that involves deliberate exposure to forge different bodily associations, trauma-informed therapy, outer group contact to forge new associations, implicit bias training, etc.). Even when we regard

---

[29] The need to more actively reflect on our inherited sociocultural values and goals, and not just when we're experiencing negative emotions, is discussed in terms of wisdom and self-regulation in Stichter (2024).

emotions as important, there's still a tendency toward dismissal of recalcitrant emotions as being significant (after all, we've judged them to be recalcitrant), but an embodied perspective ought to push that there's still work to be done in changing the source of that recalcitrance.[30] In other words, even in the case of recalcitrant emotions the emotional responses are still reliable sources for the acquisition of self-knowledge.

4.6 Reliable Processes vs Fallible Feelings

As the discussion of outlaw emotions highlights, emotions involve appraisals that reference external (i.e., the situation) and internal (i.e., goals+) targets. Because of this, it's important to point out differences in the reliability of these appraisals, in addition to differences in the reliability of the underlying emotional processes versus our conscious feelings of them. Sreenivasan (2018) has a helpful discussion of emotions and what we're justified in believing as a result of our emotional responses (assuming we know what they are). In his discussion, he's considering what emotions might justify us in believing about things external to ourselves, but we can adapt this to bring out the fact that emotional appraisals are rooted in our goals+ and to focus on what is often left out of these discussions – what do these emotional responses justify us in believing about ourselves? So, Sreenivasan (2018, 502) provides, as an example, an "epistemic thesis" (ET) about fear such that:

> (ET) Other things being equal, a person who is afraid of something is justified in believing that this thing is dangerous.

However, the emotional response isn't just an appraisal of an external object as to whether it might be dangerous in-and-of-itself, as the emotional response is also an appraisal relative to our goals+. Thus, we can adapt this to include claims about self-knowledge (SET), and generate the thesis that:

> (SET) Other things being equal, a person who is afraid of something is justified in believing that they have goals+ that could be threatened by it.

Crucially, emotional appraisals need to be understood in terms relative to one's goals+, not just in terms of properties of things external to oneself.

---

[30] Many discussions of outlaw emotions involve debates about whether emotions offer defeasible reasons for challenging ideology. One side effect of this seems to be that if the reason is "defeated" then the emotional response that gave rise to it is seen as irrelevant. But given what these emotional responses indicate about oneself, it wouldn't make sense to just dismiss the emotional response entirely because of the presence of a justified (even if false) conflicting belief.

What grounds the justification of beliefs arising out of a fear response?[31] Sreenivasan (2018, 504–505) draws on reliabilism in arguing that one option is that:

> (ET) is made true by fear's reliability as a disposition. In particular, the disposition of fear reliably tracks the presence of danger in the subject's environment. Of course, this is only reliability for the most part and in general ... These and other qualifications will affect which conditions have to obtain for 'other things to be equal.'

He goes on to note that it's likely that some other emotions can be grounded in this kind of evolutionary explanation of reliability. So, the claim is that because fear reliably, though not infallibly, tracks threats that the experience of fear generates a justified belief (though still limited by the "all other things being equal" caveat) that there is a threat. This threat provides a presumptive reason to attend to the presence of the threat and to guide our action accordingly.[32]

This argument about the reliability of some emotional processes with respect to evaluative appraisals of external objects and events can be pushed further when we think in terms about the reliability of emotional processes with respect to what justified beliefs (other things being equal) we can acquire about ourselves. While emotional responses can involve misappraisals of a situation, and responses the body prepares for the situation may not be all-things-considered the best responses to take (e.g., the responses may have been impaired by trauma, or they reflect internalized oppression from social structures), such responses can still provide reliable insight into our goals+. The idea here is that you're unlikely to have had an emotional response if you didn't have a goal that was potentially

---

[31] Here Sreenivasan is responding to an argument by Brady (2013) that the fear response does not provide any justification for a belief that something is threatening but rather merely provides motivation for further investigation about whether one is in any danger. Brady's worry is that merely feeling fear shouldn't be taken as self-justifying the belief that the fear is apt.

[32] Though, as Sreenivasan (2018, 503) points out, when it comes to emotions generating a reason for action, "there is a difference between a reason's being defeated and an emotion's failing to generate a reason in the first place (e.g., because it has misfired)." For example, fear of a snake gives you a reason to avoid it, but that reason might be "defeated" by a stronger reason to approach it to capture it (perhaps because of a monetary reward or to keep it from threatening anyone else). But fear of a rubber snake, which you initially took to be a real snake, does not give you a reason to avoid it – the emotional response in this sense 'misfired' in that it involved a mistaken appraisal of the "snake" (and the rubber snake was never truly relevant to one's goals+). This is also a reason why he prefers to formulate his "epistemic thesis" (ET) in terms of a belief being justified "other things being equal" rather than in terms of "defeasible reasons," so that it's broader to accommodate both a reason being defeated but also an emotional misfire that never generated a genuine reason in the first place. Though an emotion "misfiring" in his sense is more specifically that one of the inputs to the appraisal of the situation (e.g., the snake taken to be real rather than fake) is mistaken. However, the fear response would still be apt insofar as you took the snake to be real.

supported or thwarted (even though this may be a goal that you weren't fully aware of or that you don't fully endorse). For example, your fear at the sight of a rubber snake may involve a false belief about it being a threat, but not a false belief that you care (to some extent) about self-preservation. So, assuming you know your emotional state, you can acquire further self-knowledge about your underlying goals+ upon which that emotional process was based.[33]

Having said that, it will help to return to some earlier points that while self-knowledge of our emotional states is a path to greater self-knowledge of our goals+, because our emotional responses are reliable at tracking threats or opportunities relative to our goals+, we are often less than reliable at knowing our own emotional states. As Roberts (1995, 329) nicely sums up in a discussion of emotion and knowing oneself:

> If emotions are states of the self and indeed states quite directly related to the self's core, and the feeling of an emotion is a conscious, quasi-perceptual awareness of being in such a state, emotional feelings are a very special and important form of self-knowledge. To the extent that we are "out of touch with our feelings" (for "feelings" read "emotions"; for "be in touch with" read "feel") – to the extent that we do not feel the resentment, envy, anxiety, and fear that characterize us; or do feel a compassion, joy, and gratitude that do not characterize us; to the extent that the objects of the emotions we feel are not quite the objects of our real emotions – to that extent we are blind to ourselves.

So, our feelings (in terms of emotional consciousness or awareness) might be "out of touch" with our underlying emotional processes. As we've already noted in much of the research we've referenced so far, people vary to what extent they're in touch with their bodily and affective states. We'll go on to argue that part of the reason for that is that bodily and affective self-knowledge can be difficult to acquire, but also that we can improve our abilities to acquire this knowledge.

5 Self-Knowledge Can Be Difficult to Acquire

Perhaps it might still be assumed that figuring out our goals and what matters most to us is something that is mostly transparent, or given, most of the time. If you know what you want, then the only thing to deliberate about is how to get it. If that were the case, then we wouldn't need to acquire emotional self-knowledge

---

[33] In later sections, we'll argue that we can improve emotional self-knowledge through skill and deliberate practice. Knowing our underlying goals when these aren't clear to us may also involve inference from knowledge of our emotional responses and details of the context in which they occur. While we think these are important elements for acquiring self-knowledge of our goals+, we don't take this to be an exhaustive account, and further research is needed here.

to know our own goals, values, interests, cares, and concerns. However, we take there to be good reasons for Benjamin Franklin's quote about how hard it is to know oneself. After all, in addition to the social factors and nonconscious states discussed earlier, it is widely accepted among philosophers and psychologists that our access to our own mental states is often unreliable (Schwitzgebel 2008; Williamson 2000). It is not only that our beliefs or reasons are at times difficult to discern or just plain confabulated (Nisbett and Wilson 1977), but that even our knowledge of our own conscious visual and emotional experience isn't all that straightforward (Dennett 1993, 2002; Noe 2004; O'Regan 1992; Schwitzgebel 2008, 2012). Moreover, the extensive literature on implicit biases and their frequent inconsistency with sincerely held beliefs about one's own character, values, and principles also lead us to doubt that knowing ourselves, our priorities, and values is a straightforward affair (Cassam 2014; Saul 2013; Schwitzgebel 2012). The claims that we want to endorse are that we need to know what we feel in order to know what we care about, and also that knowing what we feel isn't always an easy thing to do. Put otherwise: emotional self-knowledge reveals to us our goals +, but acquisition of emotional self-knowledge can sometimes be difficult. Fortunately, there's also the possibility of practice and training for improving self-knowledge (as we will cover in the final section).

Let's go back to our example of Alan. Notice that there are lots of reasons why it might not be so easy for Alan to detect the quality of his own emotions regarding writing or clinical work – maybe Alan has been raised by a novelist and academic for whom value has always been placed primarily on the written and published word. Or, perhaps, Alan was raised in a family where physical labor, above all else, bears status and intellectual pursuits are considered soft or feminine. Maybe Alan comes from a community that thinks that men should never cry and only women should show emotion or do any kind of emotional work. These are not, in our opinion, simple contextual factors to separate out from one's own emotional experience, and they are also not such uncommon beliefs for people in our culture to hold about emotions.

The claim here is that because emotions are developed and experienced in a specific familial, social, and cultural context, the having and knowing of them is not simply a straightforward matter. The fact is that the having and expressing of emotion is not something that simply happens in a biological, bottom-up manner but, rather, unfolds in a social, cultural, and normative context (Barrett 2017; Griffiths & Scarantino 2005; Mesquita 2022; Parkinson 2019). We should note that even the most ardent biological essentialist about emotions admits that emotions occur in a social context (Ekman & Davidson 1994). The nature/nurture debate is at this point much more sophisticated than a simple answer: nature or nurture (Mallon and Stitch 2000).

The fact that emotions and their expression exist in a cultural and normative landscape makes it the case that we not only feel emotions but also have beliefs about which emotions we are supposed to feel – that is, which emotions are sanctioned, for whom, and in what circumstances. Crying at a wedding (if you're a woman) is okay, but crying at a conference? Not so much. Elation at a football game is okay, but at a funeral? Not so much. Expressions of emotions are apt for being governed by cultural and group norms – emotions, after all, it has been claimed, can be conceptualized as scripts (Eickers forthcoming; Eickers & Prinz 2020), as social signals (Griffiths and Scarantino 2005; Parkinson 2019) as being both "inside us" and "between us" (Mesquita 2022), and are not simply fixed but adjust in response to experience (Barrett 2017). As was made clear by our discussion of outlaw emotions earlier, knowing what we "really feel" is complicated because of the myriad of ways that our feelings are governed by rules, expectations, socially constructed meanings, and develop as the result of innumerable interpersonal experiences in which our expression of emotion, and thus our beliefs about whether it is okay to feel an emotion or not, itself may have been cause for acceptance or scorn. And this is not even to mention the fact that, in general, we live in a culture that has long thought of emotions as suspect, dangerous, and womanly, thus undermining the development of even basic, but substantive, skills related to acquiring emotional self-knowledge.

Let's return again to our example of Alan – if Alan was socialized to believe that emotions, aside from anger or rage, are for women (Miller 2012), then even the uninhibited, full experience of certain emotions will be difficult for Alan to have. So, let's say that Alan receives negative feedback from his professor on a paper and Alan's spontaneous reaction tends toward sadness or anguish. Those emotions may be automatically inhibited, suppressed, or hidden. Further, the hint of such unsanctioned emotions may also be accompanied by reproachment, fear, or self-doubt. Now Alan's experience of his professor's negative feedback consists of hidden or invisible anguish mixed with fear and self-reproachment. But this admixture of emotion is ill-suited to guide Alan's self-knowledge regarding the negative feedback from the professor or the value that the paper has for him. After all, Alan's emotional experience may not be about the negative feedback or paper but an enculturated response to his feeling forbidden emotions.[34] So, is it easy for Alan to use his emotions to figure out his

---

[34] It might be that some cases of emotions "leading us astray" may be more accurately characterized as our cultural attitudes leading us astray about how to view our emotions. It might lead to a misattribution of affect that is found with those low in the ability to differentiate their emotions.

cares and concerns regarding the feedback or paper? To figure out which emotions are signals of which values for Alan, Alan needs to be able to feel what he feels in response to his circumstances, to notice what he feels, to think about what he feels, and to figure out if this corresponds to his all things considered judgment of the situation, and maybe to do these things iteratively. In this way, the acquisition of self-knowledge concerning one's own emotions is a far from straightforward affair.

Our position is that emotional self-knowledge is indispensable for acquiring self-knowledge of our values, cares, and concerns – for knowing what really matters to us. We need emotional self-knowledge as a guide to self-regulation, decision-making, goal setting, action planning, self-understanding, and the detection of normative features of objects, events, and people in the world. For these reasons, it seems important to us that we move from a position of deficit to a position of abundance, or at least adequacy, when it comes to this kind of knowledge. It's important to note that we are not claiming that what one feels can never be mistaken or needs to be taken immediately at face value or that one must endorse every implication of every emotion. We claim, simply, that emotional self-knowledge is necessary for guiding multiple fundamental aspects of human life and that the acquisition of it is something that we ought to find ways to achieve, even though it can be difficult to do.

5.1 Emotional Awareness Can Be Improved with Deliberate Practice

In the sections that follow, we will review several strands of evidence that indicate that knowledge of our own bodily and affective experiences is something that can be improved through deliberate practice (Erikson 2008). That is, we can improve our ability to know the origin, meaning, kind, and quality of our own bodily and emotional experiences by intentionally and regularly trying to know those experiences more completely. We take it that this possibility of improvement entails that our knowledge of our bodily and affective experiences is not at ceiling. If the now-outdated Cartesian position that our minds are transparent to ourselves were true, then it would mean that our experiences are known to us immediately insofar as they are experienced by us (Descartes, 1641). At least insofar as our qualitative experiences concerning internal bodily sensations and emotions are concerned, these states would be self-luminous. But certainly, if knowledge, awareness, or contact with our own lived experiences can improve with effort and practice, then it cannot be the case that such states are known to us automatically and fully.

We will argue that better access to our mental states and traits comes about through the exercise of skill. We agree with Rolla (2018, 736, emphasis his) that an implication of an enactivist approach is that "self-knowledge is not *given*, it is the outcome of a skillful access." We think that a significant amount of self-knowledge is gained by skillful access, and we will sketch the beginnings of an account of this next. However, we do not claim that all self-knowledge is necessarily acquired via skillful access. We are open to pluralism about self-knowledge, in this respect.[35] We will begin by providing an overview of skill acquisition and deliberate practice, before reviewing evidence that people can practice to improve their access to their bodily and emotional states, thus increasing their emotional self-knowledge.

5.2 An Overview of Skill and Deliberate Practice

In the previous sections, we have argued that emotional self-knowledge is a type of self-knowledge that is special in that it reveals our goals, values, interests, cares, and concerns. On our view, emotional self-knowledge is best construed as a kind of self-knowledge that arises from attention to, or contact with, embodied appraisals that are rooted in interoceptive predictions. In this way, emotional self-knowledge is a kind of self-knowledge that is about ourselves as organisms (as well as persons). We have claimed that, for various reasons, emotional self-knowledge is not immediately given but, rather, can be difficult to achieve. And we have also suggested that such knowledge can be improved or calibrated. Indeed, the preliminary evidence presented earlier suggests that nonreactive contact with, attention to, and articulation of one's own affective and bodily states allows for improvements in bodily self-awareness and subsequent mental health. As such, we contend that acquisition of affective and bodily self-knowledge can be improved through deliberate practice and, in this way, may be best thought of as a skill (Fridland & Stichter 2021).

Here, we would like to provide a preliminary sketch of the kind of skill that we have in mind. When it comes to conceptualizing the skills of acquiring emotional self-knowledge, we find it useful to appeal to Ellen Fridland's

---

[35] The focus on skill may help to resolve a tension between those who want to claim that self-knowledge is immediate (Armstrong 1993), and those like Cassam (2014) who claim that self-knowledge is a cognitive achievement (via inference), as the ease by which we may come to know our emotions is likely a product of being skilled (Rolla 2018, 736). It's part of the development of skill that things should become less effortful, but it's no less a cognitive achievement for that reason (Sosa 2007). However, we don't intend to debate here whether our skill approach counts as a form of "inferentialism" on Cassam's view. While the main claims we're advancing about skill, as well as the importance of knowing one's emotional and somatic states, don't seem to follow merely from a commitment to inferentialism, we nevertheless leave it open to defenders of that approach to provide an alternative explanation.

tripartite account of embodied skill. According to Fridland (2020), motor skills are best construed as functions from intentions to actions that are implemented by control structures that have been developed through deliberate practice. Those control structures, when it comes to motor skills, are identified at three different levels: strategic, attentional, and motor (Fridland, 2014, 2020, 2021). In her view, deliberate practice accounts for the development of control structures at each of these levels and for the integration of control structures between levels (Fridland 2014, 2017, 2019, 2020). The strategic level is the level of intentions, and Fridland (2014, 2020, 2021) contends that as skilled agents develop their skills, they improve not only in their motor coordination or speed but also in the way in which they conceive of their task, attend to their task, intervene on their task, and retain flexibility over their task in a moment-to-moment way. In this way, skills remain both intelligent and automatic (Fridland 2014, 2017, 2019, 2020).

For our purposes, we can use this tripartite model of skilled control to reflect on the nature of emotional self-knowledge. At the level of strategic control, that is, the level that is concerned with the specific plans and intentions of the agent, we can see that emotional self-knowledge would require the development of a plan or intention to attend to one's emotional states – to turn toward, make contact with, explore, name, or investigate one's feelings. For example, one may have an intention that guides the practice of naming one's strong emotions, or noticing the more nuanced qualities of one's own bodily experiences. If acquiring emotional self-knowledge involves skillfulness, we should expect that these intentions themselves become more fine-grained and appropriate the more epistemically skilled one becomes.

On Fridland's model of skill, attentional control structures are also developed through deliberate practice (2014, 2020). Attention, according to Fridland, is semantically coherent with intention but outstrips the content of intention. Put otherwise, intention sets targets for attention, but attention then develops in a way that surpasses the task as specified by the intention. In this way, we may think of having an intention to, for example, name our more intense emotions, and that intention guides our attention to those intense emotions. However, in being so guided, attention itself grows more sensitive to the more fine-grained features and characteristics of the emotion. In the end, our ability to attend to the emotion will outstrip in fineness of grain our intention to attend to the emotion. However, as stated earlier, the intention also evolves through skill learning as well, and so, though these two control elements are separable, their development is still integrated in important ways. In fact, when it comes to emotional self-knowledge, it seems that a lot of the action is exactly at the level of attention control together with strategic control.

Of course, since we are thinking about emotional and epistemic skills here and not motor skills, the level of motor control from Fridland's model will not map on directly. However, we propose that affective control may be an appropriate substitute for motor control when it comes to the lowest level of control relevant for skills of emotional self-knowledge. Moreover, if there is a level of affective control that develops with skills for acquiring emotional self-knowledge, this could further help us to understand the direct mental health benefits of this kind of knowledge.

As a preliminary suggestion, we are inclined to conjecture that since emotional self-knowledge requires attention to, contact with, recognition of, and exploration of one's own emotional experiences, and because such investigation requires an ability to regulate emotional reactivity, then this, in and of itself, may counter some of our more unhealthy automatic emotional reactions. These immediate emotional reactions include things like the tendency to avoid, deny, project, or inhibit our emotions. In this way, tolerating our emotions for the purpose of investigating them requires a kind of nonreactive attention which may itself transform or adjust the lower-level arousal that accompanies our emotional reactions.[36] If this is correct, then skills for acquiring emotional self-knowledge develop at three levels – strategic, attentional, and affective – and together provide us with a way of conceptualizing our growing ability to know ourselves as embodied organisms.

This skills-based lens through which to understand our relationship to affective and bodily information provides us with an alternative view of our emotional life as a valuable aspect of self-knowledge to be cultivated and investigated rather than overlooked, ignored, or managed. This view of emotional self-knowledge also has significant implications for education, psychotherapy, and even for our general conception of what is required for living well.

5.3 Interoceptive Awareness and Mindfulness

Having laid out an account of skill and how it might apply to improving access to our bodily and emotional states, we next provide preliminary evidence that interoceptive accuracy can indeed be improved through deliberate practice. First off, as we discussed in an earlier section, some forms of mindful awareness can improve interoceptive accuracy by engaging in the practice of identifying, as well as naming, particular bodily sensations. So, this can be described as happening at the level of strategic control in skill, when we intend to practice

---

[36] See Stichter (2020) for an example of the need to keep negative emotions, such as distress, at a manageable level – where they are neither avoided completely nor experienced with such an overwhelming intensity that they induce defensive reactions.

better identifying bodily sensations. Second, some skill development seems to inherently involve improvement in interoception, as expert dancers and musicians exhibit increased interoceptive abilities (Christensen et al. 2018; Schirmer-Mokwa et al. 2015). In these skill domains, practice is improving more than just motor control. Furthermore, it has been found that contemplative practices such as meditation over a prolonged period of time can improve introspective accuracy as measured by heartbeat detection (Bornemann & Singer 2017). This is the study discussed earlier that also found that increases in interoceptive accuracy were inversely correlated with alexithymia, a condition that is characterized by a deficit in emotional awareness. That is, decreases in alexithymia were related to increases in bodily awareness. A second study has found that performing a 20-minute body scan every day over a period of 8 weeks significantly improves interoceptive accuracy (Fischer, Messner, & Pollatos 2017). Other studies have shown that interoceptive awareness can be improved by bodily self-focus, such as gazing into a mirror (Ainley et. al. 2012) or looking at a photograph of oneself (Maister & Tsakiris 2013; Ainley et. al. 2013). These studies provide preliminary evidence that practicing focused, calm attention toward one's own bodily sensations can result in more accurate detection of interoceptive signals. Furthermore, some studies have shown improved interoceptive awareness by drawing one's "attention to the narrative aspects of the self, such as one's name or the names of significant others, and that this increase is independent of baseline levels of interoceptive awareness" (Ainley et. al. 2013). Combining these results with the conclusions earlier relating interoceptive accuracy to emotional awareness helps us to appreciate that awareness of one's internal bodily signals and, thus, emotional perception and emotional regulation are not stagnant traits but at least somewhat modifiable features of one's psychology. This line of research supports our contention that bodily information is relevant for the emotional awareness and identification required for coming to know our values, priorities, cares, and concerns. Specifically, the research on interoception gives us reason to believe that increased detection of bodily signals is importantly related to awareness of one's feelings or emotions – which provides us with better information for setting meaningful and authentic goals in line with our most cherished values, wishes, desires, and concerns.

An additional practice that can improve our emotional awareness can be seen by noting the fact that most so-called "third-wave" cognitive behavioral psychotherapeutic approaches use mindfulness and yoga as key treatment interventions. That is, approaches like ACT (Acceptance Commitment Therapy, Hayes et al. 2009), DBT (Dialectical Behavioral Therapy, Dimeff & Linehan 2001), CFT (Compassion Focused therapy, Gilbert 2010), and trauma-informed psychotherapy (Herman 1992; Van der Kolk 1994), which are fast becoming best-practices in clinical psychology, all rely on methods that increase the client's ability to notice, make contact with, and accept their affective and bodily experiences. Mindfulness-based practices use nonjudgmental and compassionate awareness of the body and the breath as a means to remain in the present moment. Often this type of mindfulness work requires investigating by training attention to the nature of one's bodily and affective experiences as they arise to develop the ability to tolerate, accept, and explore with equanimity the quality and nature of what can often be painful or unpleasant bodily experiences. Further, even more traditional CBT (cognitive behavioral therapy) interventions use breathing strategies, grounding techniques, and interventions like progressive muscle relaxation in addition to reframing, reappraisal, and challenging beliefs to decrease symptoms of common psychopathologies such as anxiety and panic (Jongsma 2021). In all, for our purposes, what's relevant to notice is that these psychotherapeutic interventions all have in common the goal of increasing a person's contact with, knowledge of, and acceptance of their own bodily sensations and emotional states via practice.

5.4 Emotional Granularity and Differentiation

There is also evidence of practices that improve awareness of one's emotional states. One way in which we can improve our knowledge of the nature and quality of our own emotional experiences is by putting them into words (i.e., a form of strategic control, like the ways in which we can do this with bodily experiences). The process of attending to, examining, describing, and labeling our affective states has the potential to increase emotional granularity, or, as Lindquist and Barrett (2008) define it, the ability to represent emotional experiences with precision and specificity. Emotional granularity and emotional differentiation (as discussed earlier) are often used interchangeably to refer to the phenomenon of differentiating emotional experiences with different fineness of grain. Bonar et al. (2023, 23–24) highlight the relevance of emotion differentiation given that emotions are appraisals of situations and help prepare us for action, such that:

> Nearly all theoretical accounts of emotion agree that emotions are most adaptive when they are highly differentiated and specific to a given situation. Decades of research demonstrate that individuals differ widely in how discretely they experience their emotions, with some experiencing emotions as categorically distinct (e.g., anger vs. fear vs. disgust) and others as more diffuse states (e.g., unpleasantness).

A more diffuse state is usually referred to as a mood, where moods have a particular valenced feel (i.e., positive or negative), but lack a specific appraisal of the cause or source of it, and as a result do not tend toward a particular action in response (though see Mendelovici 2013; Bordini 2017; Stephan 2017).

Not only do people differ from each other when it comes to their ability to make such fine-grained emotional distinctions, but the same person's capacity for emotional differentiation may be different at different times (Erbas et al. 2018, 2021) and seems to improve with age (Carstensen et al. 2000). Crucially, people's abilities for emotional differentiation are positively correlated with important psychological, social, and health outcomes. For instance, people who are high on emotional differentiation have been found to drink less in stressful circumstances (Kashdan et al. 2010) and to be less likely to retaliate aggressively to a perceived injury (Pond et al. 2012). Additionally, people low in their ability for emotional differentiation are more likely to suffer from an array of mental health disorders (Kashdan et al. 2015), including depression (Demiralp et al. 2012), social anxiety (Kashdan & Farmer 2014), eating disorders (Selby et al. 2014), and borderline personality disorder (Suvak et al. 2011).

Since emotions are states that tell us something important about our relationship to our circumstances, goals, others, and ourselves (Barrett 2017; Clore et al. 2001; Damasio 1999; Maeise 2014; Schwartz 2011), then being able to more accurately identify our own emotional states will help us to classify not only their intrinsic qualities but also their informational connections, including the state's origin or cause. This would then provide us with the opportunity to more appropriately respond to the emotion (Barrett 2017), as well as respond more effectively to the situation. For example, understanding that a bad feeling is really the fear of losing a loved one can help us to assess the appropriateness of the feeling, and to act on it in a more deliberate, congruent, and authentic manner (Rogers 1995).[37] This would be an example of changing a diffuse negative mood into a specific emotional experience, and thus improving the information that such an affective response can provide. Negative moods can be especially problematic insofar as they are unpleasant, and although you know they indicate that something is wrong, without further insight into the source of it, you don't know how to respond to fix the problem, thus leaving you sitting with unpleasant affect which doesn't easily dissipate (and this can have negative

---

[37] This type of ability for congruent behavior has been closely tied to mental well-being. Of note is that the opposite of contact with and access to one's own experience – what is known in clinical psychology as "experiential avoidance" or the unwillingness to remain in contact with aversive private experience, including bodily sensations, emotions, thoughts, memories, and behavioral predispositions (Hayes et al. 1996) – is also highly correlated with negative mental health outcomes (see Chawla & Pstafin 2007 for review).

consequences for cognition and behavior). Those higher in emotion differentiation can experience specific negative emotions which help them to know how to respond to the specific situation (insofar as the cause or source is correctly identified), rather than experiencing a merely diffuse negative mood that doesn't provide action guidance beyond either prompting one to seek to understand the cause of it (i.e., approach, adaptive) or to try to ignore it or get distracted from it (i.e., avoidance, maladaptive).

Important for our purposes is the fact that people can improve in their ability to make fine-grained distinctions concerning their emotional experiences. Kashdan et al. (2015, 12) claim that emotion differentiation "transcends any single psychological problem, serving as a skill that facilitates psychological and social well-being." In support of this, in one set of studies, Cameron, Payne, and Doris (2013) showed how being skilled at emotion differentiation can help prevent irrelevant emotions, like disgust, from impacting moral judgments. Cameron et al. found that those skilled in emotion differentiation were not affected in their moral judgments by the priming of incidental disgust (which was done by exposing participants to disgusting images) prior to reading a story that involved a moral transgression. Those who were skilled at differentiating their emotions were able to recognize that they were feeling disgust and that the source of it was exposure to the images, and so it didn't impact their subsequent moral judgment about the moral transgression in the story. By contrast, those who could not differentiate their affective state had more severe reactions to the moral transgression. This diffuse negative affective state colored their moral judgment, as those who were unskilled ended up misattributing their negativity to the moral transgression (as diffuse affective states have no clear source), thus leading to a harsher overall judgment about the transgression. This happened despite the fact that they had been previously warned that disgust could have this effect. But one would have to recognize that they were feeling not just bad but more specifically disgust for that information to be relevant.

Furthermore, as evidence that one can be more or less skilled with respect to emotion differentiation, in a follow-up study, Cameron et al. provided participants with some training in emotion differentiation, and this helped to counter the influence of incidental emotions. Cameron et al. (2013, 722) stated that these "instructions were designed to encourage differentiated emotional introspection by focusing people on subtle differences between their emotions." The training involved participants being instructed on how emotions have important nuances in how they feel, and then participants were asked to reflect on a variety of emotional responses that they might be having when they were later shown some highly emotional imagery. Vedernikova, Kuppens, and Erbas (2021) did a similar intervention and also reported that such training improved people's ability to differentiate their emotions.

Other evidence of skill might be seen in an interesting pattern where there tends to be a dip in children's ability to differentiate their emotions during adolescence (Nook et al. 2018). Young children tend to report having only singular emotions, whereas adolescents report multiple emotions co-occurring. This change from singular to co-occurring emotions would make it more difficult to differentiate the emotions one is experiencing, and this presumably would account for a dip in emotion differentiation in adolescents as they struggle to understand their more complex emotional experiences. Though Nook et al. (2018) suggest that over time that "emotion differentiation may rise within this period as young adults learn to separate coexperienced emotions using increasingly defined emotion concepts." As skill involves progressively tackling more difficult challenges, with the greater complexity in the task of differentiating co-occurring emotions it should be expected that it would take additional time and practice to master.

Additionally, Van der Gucht et al. (2019) have shown that a traditional mindfulness training program where individuals apply nonjudgmental awareness to their own bodily and affective states can improve people's abilities to differentiate their own emotional experiences.[38] Lastly, it has been found that experiential sampling itself, that is, the practice of attending to, describing, and labeling one's own emotional experiences, can improve emotional differentiation of both positive and negative emotions in clinical populations (Widdershoven et al. 2019) and among healthy adults (Hoemann et al. 2021). Taken together, these preliminary findings suggest that there are possibilities for improving one's ability to precisely and accurately identify one's own emotional states by attending to and describing one's experiences. In this way, we can see that cultivating the appropriate epistemic and intrapersonal orientation toward our own emotional states is something that we can practice and become skilled at.

5.5 Skills and Self-Transformation

One further unique feature of our account of skilled access to affective and bodily states is that it provides reasons to expect that at least some ways in which we acquire greater affective/bodily self-knowledge could also involve qualitative changes in how we experience ourselves (even if they don't lead to

---

[38] However, we aren't claiming that mindfulness is always good, but rather that it is one way in which we might be able to develop emotional granularity. For some worries about adverse effects of mindfulness practices, see Britton (2019), Lindahl et al. (2017), and Simon, Shortreed, & Rossom (2022).

such changes on every occasion). Granted, this is a hypothesis derived from what we know about skill acquisition leading to qualitative changes in experience, such as with the development of motor control, so while we expect skilled access to lead to qualitative changes in how we experience our affective/bodily states, this would require further empirical research. Nevertheless, there is some promising evidence along these lines that we'll explore in the following sections.

That skills in acquiring affective/bodily self-knowledge also leads to transformations in the self shouldn't be surprising given the, seemingly under-appreciated, fact that all skill development involves some degree of self-transformation. It's not uncommon to view skill acquisition as akin to acquiring a tool to perform a task where the acquired skilled is just a new tool in the toolkit for getting things done. Just like you pick up the tool when it's useful, you exercise your skill when it's relevant, but the rest of the time it's stored away and inert. While a tool is literally external to the self, and skill development is largely an internal process, nevertheless there's a tendency to treat skill acquisition in this externalized sense where the acquisition or exercise of it doesn't change you in any fundamental respect any more than buying and using a hammer would.

However, acquiring a skill just is a process of internal self-transformation, even if only a small degree at times, as it's a matter of changing the way you think, perceive, experience and interact with your environment. Acquiring a skill involves adopting a goal of self-improvement, as you're adopting standards of performance which will take some effort for you to reach. This goal then affects your motivation, as you'll be motivated to take actions to improve your abilities (i.e., deliberate practice), and it will also shape your affective responses in terms of getting positive or negative affective feedback regarding how well you're performing. In other words, you're going to come to care about how you're performing in some domain because of setting yourself the goal of acquiring a skill.

Furthermore, skill acquisition will change the way you perceive situations. Take a simple example of a chess board and how an expert and novice chess player can see the same pieces on the board but won't see the same moves to make to win the game. It's not an embellishment to say that the expert and the novice see the situation differently, as Fridland (2017) points out that research has demonstrated differences between experts and novices in their use of visual search strategies – that there are differences in what they're perceiving and thus what perceptual information is guiding their choice of action – for they're attending to different aspects of the board to guide their next move. Fridland (2017, 149) claims that:

experts employ fewer visual fixations than non-experts (inter alia they attend to fewer locations) and those fixations last for longer periods of time than the visual fixations of non-experts. As such, we can say that the selective attention of experts differs from that of non-experts along at least three dimensions: frequency, location, and duration.

So, it's not the case that experts and novices have the same perceptual input but differ in the inferences they draw from that input, as it's rather that they are starting with different perceptions of the situation. Experts know where to look to gain information that is most relevant for guiding their actions and their attention is directed to these areas automatically. In addition, Fridland (2017, 155) notes that "studies of perceptual learning show that with training and practice, individuals become able to detect perceptual patterns that are unitized into meaningful components," and that these patterns aren't perceived by those with less experience.

This can also be helpfully cached out in terms of shaping your perception of affordances – what possibilities for action exist in your current environment. What an environment affords you is a joint product of features of the environment itself and your goals+ and abilities. What a situation affords will be shaped to some extent by our cares and concerns (i.e., the values that might be realized or undermined in a situation). For example, walking through a park and seeing a lone individual by a chess board might be perceived as a chance to enjoy a game of chess, or an opportunity to practice your skills, at least for those who desire to play. What possibilities an environment might afford are further shaped to some extent by our own abilities, skills, and expertise. A steep mountainside might afford an opportunity to go rock climbing, but only for those who have some skill in it. As one progressively develops one's degree of skill, then, new possibilities for action can be seen.

Another type of transformation can be seen in the way motor control develops as a result of attentive deliberate practice involving qualitative changes in the movement itself. Take, for example, finger position for a beginning piano player, or posture for a beginner in yoga. What begins as a diffuse sort of blunt motor control can become more refined/fine-grained as one practices the relevant movements in the relevant ways (as in, the movement doesn't stay the same while control is applied but practice changes the movement itself). The idea is that there is a process of motor control that becomes refined with practice and that allows for further refinements of motor control as one continues to practice. The parallel would be that as one deliberately attends to one's affective experience in the right way, one can refine that experience through one's understanding of it (the experience of anger/disgust is then a different experience from the experience of diffuse negative affect and the experience of righteous indignation would differ from the less fine-grained state of anger, etc.). This then allows further fine-grained refinements to take hold. So, on the skill view, there's a feedback loop of experiential refinements that transforms the affective experience as one experiences it in reflective and attentive ways.

These changes might be minor with a small degree of skill development but can also be quite significant over time if one continues to improve one's skillfulness. Psychologists studying the development of expertise have noted that the kind of change people undergo with skill development can be quite sophisticated, and Feltovich et al. (2006, 57) claim that the development of skill and expertise involves "a complex *construct* of adaptations of mind and body, which include substantial self-monitoring and control mechanisms, to task environments in service of representative task goals and activities." Sosniak (1987) did an extensive study of 120 experts across 20 domains and found that the development of such high degrees of skillfulness involved a self-transformation on the part of the learner. One example group Sosniak (1987, 521) studied were concert pianists, and he remarked that:

> the essential change in the pianists' successful learning was in how they understood their experiences. The change was both qualitative and evolutionary. As the pianists developed skills, aspirations, commitments, and identities, they reorganized and reinterpreted their experiences. Over a period of about seventeen years the pianists were gradually reoriented and transformed.

So, in becoming more skillful in acquiring affective/bodily self-knowledge, it's plausible to expect that the development of these skills will lead to some changes, perhaps even dramatic transformations, in the way in which we experience ourselves.

5.6 Transforming Emotional Experiences

For evidence that improved emotional skills will lead to qualitative changes in our emotional experiences, we'll return to some further implications stemming from the research on emotion differentiation. Cameron et al. (2013, 720) helpfully draw our attention to how the ability to differentiate one's emotions results in a qualitative change in one's affective experiences:

> unskilled emotion differentiators may simply report that they "feel bad" (focusing on unspecified negative valence), without distinguishing between negative emotions such as disgust and anger (they would report equivalent levels of disgust and anger because they are not conceptually differentiating between the two). Unskilled emotion differentiators do not use specific emotion concepts to categorize affect into distinct emotional states, leading their affective experiences to be broad, undifferentiated, and diffuse.

Being skilled in emotion differentiation allows one to take an otherwise global and diffuse affective state (or mood), like 'I'm feeling bad,' and recognize that one is feeling a specific emotion – like feeling anger, disgust, fear, guilt, sadness, and shame. If you're unskilled, you're limited to knowing only that you feel bad. If you're skilled, you'll have acquired further self-knowledge because you also know that you're more specifically feeling disgust.

But for those able to differentiate well it's not just that you know more about what you're feeling, because you're also changing what it is that you're feeling. Those who were skilled had qualitatively different affective experiences because what they were feeling wasn't "broad, undifferentiated, and diffuse." Those who were skilled in emotion differentiation didn't have to infer that they were feeling disgust because they were already experiencing their negative affect just as disgust (rather than as a merely negatively valenced mood). The process of acquiring self-knowledge about their affective states was leading to transformations in their affective states.[39]

Those changes in affective states can further influence the way in which people respond to their environment, as seen in the way in which those skilled differentiators who knew they were experiencing disgust did not misattribute their negatively valenced affect as arising from the moral transgression in the story and thus judging it more harshly. Furthermore, this seemed to occur automatically, rather than the self-knowledge being used as an input into a deliberative process, given the speed at which participants responded to prompts about transgressions, which supports the idea that becoming more skilled in emotion differentiation leads to some transformations of the self in which they relate differently to themselves and others. While initial training in emotion differentiation might involve deliberate processes of trying to infer from a diffuse mood what discrete emotion underlies that mood, or separating out co-occurring emotions, such as when we're prompted to reflect on what exactly it is we're feeling, this deliberative step isn't needed once one's affective experiences have been transformed such that one isn't experiencing a diffuse mood in the first place. Starkey (2008, 434) makes a similar claim in distinguishing between cases of feeling anxious from cases where we conclude from observing our bodily changes that we're likely anxious, stating that in the former there's "an experiential association that joins affective and cognitive elements, not an inferential association, and as such the elements are experienced in a united way rather than merely cognitively linked." This kind of

---

[39] Our account of the skills involved with acquiring affective self-knowledge might then imply that self-knowledge is sometimes a moving target, in the sense that the process of coming to know yourself also leads to changes in yourself, such that there is something new to know about yourself.

example of a change in process as a result of becoming more skilled is also a familiar feature of accounts of skill acquisition which acknowledge that at early stages of skill acquisition learners might be explicitly following rules about how to act, but it doesn't follow that higher levels of skill development involve following ever more sophisticated rules.

Brown et al. (2021) provide further evidence for a qualitative difference in how people experience negative affect resulting from stressful situations between those who are high in negative emotion differentiation (NED) and those who are low. Their most significant finding was that those higher in NED were less likely to use disengagement strategies to cope with distress, and that:

> our findings that people higher in NED less frequently use distraction are consistent with research demonstrating that people may use distraction when they feel overwhelmed and confused by emotional experiences (e.g., Sheppes et al., 2011; 2014). Thus, rather than try to decipher their emotional experiences, they may instead disengage from them. (2021, 8)

This suggests that those low in NED have emotional experiences in which "they feel overwhelmed and confused" whereas those high in NED don't have that same feeling. The confusion those with low NED experience presumably results from them experiencing distress as a diffuse negative mood which doesn't have a clear source and doesn't indicate a particular action to take to alleviate the distress – hence the confusion. This confusion could potentially build into an "emotional cascade" which Tomko et al. (2015, 741) describe as happening when "a person experiencing negative affect (NA) ruminates intensely on the situation or NA itself, resulting in increased NA. The "cascade" is terminated only when the individual engages in dysregulated or impulsive behavior as a means of distraction from the rumination." If you don't know why you're feeling the way you are, and what you're feeling is (increasingly) unpleasant, then lacking any clear action guidance you're likely to be motivated to just disengage from that feeling entirely (via distraction), although a more adaptive response would be to seek help in gaining greater self-knowledge about one's affective experiences (e.g., see a therapist). By contrast, as Thompson et al. (2021) point out, "people high in both differentiation ability and automaticity may always have accurate information at hand, and thus use that information reflexively, regardless of urgency and other situational constraints." For those low in NED, it also likely takes more cognitive effort to try to effectively differentiate, relative to those who have practiced it and can differentiate more automatically as we see with skilled responses, and that attempt may be especially difficult to carry out in times where one is already feeling overwhelmed by emotional distress.

Here we can return to an earlier worry about the extent to which cultural upbringing and socialization teach us that emotions are irrational. Insofar as emotions aren't seen as providing us with self-knowledge and information relevant to guiding our actions, then it wouldn't be surprising if we aren't as motivated to learn how to differentiate our emotions. As a result, we're then vulnerable to feeling "overwhelmed and confused" by negative affect and to be motivated to disengage from it (since we don't know a better course of action). But not attending to our affective states just is to ignore a relevant source of information that we should be attending to in order to effectively guide our actions in situations, and this undermines their adaptive function. As Kashdan et al. (2015, 14) point out, for those low in emotion differentiation, "sensory inputs will be conceptualized in a relatively undifferentiated fashion, depriving that person of the contextualized knowledge that is required to deal with the situation at hand." In addition, we think this could then fuel a self-reinforcing belief in emotions as being irrelevant, or an unwanted distraction, to acting well if people aren't seeing a benefit from emotions when they're experiencing them. This could further undermine motivation to try to differentiate and acquire self-knowledge about one's affective states (see Thompson et al. 2021).

Another line of supporting evidence indicating a qualitative change with emotion differentiation comes from studies of affect labeling where participants who are asked to associate an emotional word with an emotional image (e.g., an angry face) experienced less distress, and that there's an underlying physiological change to account for this, compared with those who saw the image but didn't put a label to it. Lieberman et al. (2007, 421) explain that studies have shown that the "linguistic processing of the emotional aspects of an emotional image produces less amygdala activity than perceptual processing of the emotional aspects of the same image ... thus helping to alleviate emotional distress." Along the same lines, Kashdan et al. (2015, 14) "propose that emotion vocabulary words are linked to the emotion concepts that people use to conceptualize their affective experiences and to transform them into more refined, granular emotional experiences" and "[b]ecause conceptual knowledge is embodied, it can also serve to modify internal sensations from the body and reduce intense negative affect." This supports the idea that being able to put your feelings into words makes those experiences less distressing, which would account for a lesser use of disengagement strategies on the part of those more skilled in negative emotion differentiation.

Phan and Sripada (2013, 392) discuss similar results of affect labeling having the effect of reducing amygdala activity and decreasing felt negative affect. In addition, they report on studies by Herwig et al. (2010) in which they asked participants to self-reflect in one of three ways:

(1) the "think" condition: "think about yourself, reflect who you are, about your goals, etc." (2) the "feel" condition: "feel yourself, be aware about your current emotions and bodily feelings;" and (3) the "neutral" condition: "do nothing specific, just await the neutral picture" (Herwig, Kaffenberger, Jancke, & Bruhl, 2010). The authors reported that the emotion introspection "feel" condition was associated with the lowest amgydala activation and that the mental state of being aware of emotional state changes is capable of down-regulating emotional arousal, as indexed by reduced amygdala reactivity. (Phan & Sripada, 2013, 393)

This research suggests that having greater emotional self-knowledge will change what it is you're experiencing, such that the changes aren't just at the level of what is consciously felt but are also taking place at the physiological level.

It's worth noting that while affect labeling and emotion differentiation sometimes lead to noticeable physiological changes, that's not always the case. Bonar et al. (2023) found in stress response tests that while those high in NED reported less negative affect, they still had the same heightened physiological response (as measured by cardiac activity) as those lower in NED. But that's understandable as a response to stress because it wouldn't necessarily be adaptive if greater insight into one's affective experiences had the effect of reducing the body's preparedness for action. They propose that the difference in felt affect may be explained if "individuals higher in NED experienced a psychophysiological state more akin to a "challenge" state (vs. a "threat" state) during the stressor" (2023, 23). Insofar as a challenge would be perceived as more manageable than a threat, in that one views oneself as having the resources to meet the challenge (unlike a threat), this could account for both experiencing less distress when meeting a challenge while still maintaining the body's cardiovascular preparedness to handle the challenge. In support of this, Jamieson et al. (2018) found that while appraisals of situations as challenge versus threat had some overlapping physiological responses, a key difference was that challenges produced higher levels of anabolic hormones while threats produced higher levels of catabolic hormones (i.e., cortisol – which has the drawback of a prolonged stress response). Here we see a connection between changes in appraisals leading to changes in feeling, including underlying physiological responses, and differences in action tendencies (as challenges can be approached but threats should be avoided). So, the research is suggestive of gains in emotional self-knowledge leading to qualitative changes in emotional experiences, though more empirical work in this area would be helpful.

6 Conclusion

We began by laying out a puzzle of "feeling well" as to why bodily and emotional self-knowledge is so strongly associated with good mental health and well-being, along with providing empirical evidence for that association. We then tried to solve that puzzle by mapping out the connections between bodily states, emotional states, and our goals+ with an account of emotions as embodied appraisals. Emotions being embodied means that emotional responses are accompanied by physiological changes (e.g., directing attention, preparing us for action), such that self-knowledge of our bodily states helps us to acquire knowledge of our emotional states, and sometimes gives us insight into our goals+ as well. Emotions as appraisals mean that situations are appraised relative to our goals+, such that self-knowledge of our emotional states helps us to acquire knowledge of our goals+.

In doing so, we've also discussed some of the reasons why these types of self-knowledge are associated with good mental health and well-being, for example, in aiding emotion regulation, uncovering goals that aren't transparent to us, having a better understanding of our cares and concerns such that we can set more appropriate goals, and so on. However, we also noted reasons why emotional self-knowledge can be difficult to acquire. Fortunately, there's evidence that through deliberate practice we can improve our awareness of our bodily states, which by itself improves our awareness of our emotional states (e.g., mindfulness), and that there are further ways we can practice to increase our emotional self-knowledge (e.g., emotion differentiation). We outlined an account of skill that we claimed can also usefully be applied to skillful access to our bodily and emotional states. Finally, we speculated that given that improvement in skill can lead to qualitative changes in how we interact with the world, we put forward the idea (along with some preliminary evidence) that becoming more emotionally skilled will lead to qualitative changes in our emotional experiences.

Importantly, we think this is just the beginning of the story. Given that we've tried to push emotional self-knowledge in new directions, we don't consider our account to be comprehensive. In fact, we hope that it will spark a lot of interest in further exploring emotional self-knowledge and connections to self-knowledge of our goals +, and adding to, as well as correcting, the outline we've provided so far. There is surely more philosophical and empirical work to be done on this topic and we're excited to see where it leads.

References

Ainley, V., Maister, L., Brokfeld, J., Farmer, H., & Tsakiris, M. (2013). More of myself: Manipulating interoceptive awareness by heightened attention to bodily and narrative aspects of the self. *Consciousness and Cognition*, 22(4), 1231–1238.

Ainley, V., Tajadura-Jiménez, A., Fotopoulou, A., & Tsakiris, M. (2012). Looking into myself: Changes in interoceptive sensitivity during mirror self-observation. *Psychophysiology*, 49(11), 1672–1676.

Aristotle. (1941). *Nicomachean ethics* (W. D. Ross, trans.). Random House.

Armstrong, D. M. (1993). *A materialist theory of the mind*. Routledge.

Barrett, L. F. (2006). Are emotions natural kinds? *Perspectives on Psychological Science*, 1, 28–58.

Barrett, L. F. (2017). *How emotions are made: The secret life of the brain*. Pan Macmillan.

Barrett, L. F., Gross, J., Christensen, T. C., & Benvenuto, M. (2001). Knowing what you're feeling and knowing what to do about it: Mapping the relation between emotion differentiation and emotion regulation. *Cognition & Emotion*, 15(6), 713–724.

Barrett, L. F., Quigley, K. S., Bliss-Moreau, E., & Aronson, K. R. (2004). Interoceptive sensitivity and self-reports of emotional experience. *Journal of Personality and Social Psychology*, 87(5), 684–697.

Bechara, A., & Naqvi, N. (2004). Listening to your heart: Interoceptive awareness as a gateway to feeling. *Nature Neuroscience*, 7(2), 102–3.

Bechara, A., Damasio, H., Tranel, D., & Damasio, A. R. (2005). The Iowa Gambling Task and the somatic marker hypothesis: some questions and answers. *Trends in Cognitive Sciences*, 9(4), 159–162.

Betka, S., Pfeifer, G., Garfinkel, S. et al. (2018). How do self-assessment of alexithymia and sensitivity to bodily sensations relate to alcohol consumption?. *Alcoholism, Clinical and Experimental Research*, 42(1), 81–88.

Bird, G., Silani, G., Brindley, R. et al. (2010). Empathic brain responses in insula are modulated by levels of alexithymia but not autism. *Brain*, 133(5), 1515–1525.

Bonar, A. S., MacCormack, J. K., Feldman, M. J., & Lindquist, K. A. (2023). Examining the role of emotion differentiation on emotion and cardiovascular physiological activity during acute stress. *Affective Science*, 4(2), 317–331.

Bordini, D. (2017). Not in the mood for intentionalism. *Midwest Studies in Philosophy*, 41(1), 60–81.

Bornemann, B., & Singer, T. (2017). Taking time to feel our body: Steady increases in heartbeat perception accuracy and decreases in alexithymia over 9 months of contemplative mental training. *Psychophysiology*, 54(3), 469–482.

Brady, M. S. (2009). The irrationality of recalcitrant emotions. *Philosophical Studies*, 145, 413–430.

Brady, M. (2013). *Emotional insight*. Oxford University Press.

Britton, W. B. (2019). Can mindfulness be too much of a good thing? The value of a middle way. *Current Opinion in Psychology*, 28, 159–165.

Brown, B. A., Goodman, F. R., Disabato, D. J. et al. (2021). Does negative emotion differentiation influence how people choose to regulate their distress after stressful events? A four-year daily diary study. *Emotion (Washington, DC)*, 21(5), 1000–1012.

Cameron, C. D., Payne, B. K., & Doris, J. M. (2013). Morality in high definition: Emotion differentiation calibrates the influence of incidental disgust on moral judgments. *Journal of Experimental Social Psychology*, 49(4), 719–725.

Carstensen, L. L., Pasupathi, M., Mayr, U., & Nesselroade, J. R. (2000). Emotional experience in everyday life across the adult life span. *Journal of Personality and Social Psychology*, 79(4), 644–655.

Carver, C. S., & Scheier, M. F. (1990). Origins and functions of positive and negative affect: A control-process view. *Psychological Review*, 97(1), 19–35.

Cassam, Q. (2014). *Self-Knowledge for Humans*. Oxford University Press.

Chartrand, T. L., Cheng, C. M., Dalton, A. N., & Tesser, A. (2010). Nonconscious goal pursuit: Isolated incidents or adaptive self-regulatory tool. *Social Cognition*, 28(5), 569–588.

Chawla, N. & Ostafin, B. (2007). Experiential avoidance as a functional dimensional approach to psychopathology: An empirical review. *Journal of Clinical Psychology*, 63(9), 871–890.

Cholbi, M. (2019). Regret, resilience, and the nature of grief. *Journal of Moral Philosophy*, 16(4), 486–508.

Christensen, J. F., Gaigg, S. B., & Calvo-Merino, B. (2018). I can feel my heartbeat: Dancers have increased interoceptive accuracy. *Psychophysiology*, 55(4), e13008.

Clore, G. L., Gasper, K., & Garvin, E. (2001). Affect as information. In J. P. Forgas, ed., *Handbook of affect and social cognition*. Lawrence Erlbaum, pp. 121–144.

Colombetti, G. (2020). Embodied self-referentiality. *Philosophy, Psychiatry, & Psychology*, 27(1), 51–52.

Colombetti, G., & Thompson, E. (2007). The feeling body: Toward an enactive approach to emotion. In W. F. Overton, U. Müller, & J. L. Newman, eds., *Developmental Perspectives on Embodiment and Consciousness*. Psychology Press, pp. 61–84.

Craig, A. D. (2003). Interoception: The sense of the physiological condition of the body. *Current Opinion in Neurobiology*, 13(4), 500–505.

Critchley, H. D., & Garfinkel, S. N. (2017). Interoception and emotion. *Current Opinion in Psychology*, 17, 7–14.

Critchley, H. D., & Nagai, Y. (2012). How emotions are shaped by bodily states. *Emotion Review*, 4(2), 163–168.

D'Arms, J., & Jacobson, D. (2003). VIII. The significance of recalcitrant emotion (or, anti-quasijudgmentalism). *Royal Institute of Philosophy Supplement*, 52, 127–145.

D'Arms, J., & Jacobson, D. (2010). Demystifying sensibilities. In P. Goldie, ed., *Oxford handbook of philosophy of emotion*. New York: Oxford University Press, pp. 585–614.

Damasio, A. R. (1999). *The feeling of what happens: Body and emotion in the making of consciousness*. Houghton Mifflin Harcourt.

Demiralp, E., Thompson, R. J., Mata, J. et al. (2012). Feeling blue or turquoise? Emotional differentiation in major depressive disorder. *Psychological Science*, 23(11), 1410–1416.

Dennett, D. C. (1993). *Consciousness explained*. Penguin.

Dennett, D. (2002). How could I be wrong? How wrong could I be?. *Journal of Consciousness Studies*, 9(5–6), 13–16.

Deonna, J. A. (2006). Emotion, perception and perspective. *Dialectica*, 60(1), 29–46.

Deonna, J., & Teroni, F. (2012). *The emotions: A philosophical introduction*. Routledge.

Deonna, J., & Teroni, F. (2014). In What Sense Are Emotions Evaluations? In S. Roeser, & C. Todd, eds., *Emotion and value*. Oxford: Oxford University Press, pp. 15–31.

Deonna, J. A., & Teroni, F. (2022). Why are emotions epistemically indispensable?. *Inquiry*, 68(1), 1–23.

Descartes, R. (1999, first published 1641). *Discourse on method and meditations on first philosophy*. Hackett.

DeSousa, R. (1987). *The rationality of emotion*. MIT Press.

DeYoung, C. G., & Tiberius, V. (2023). Value fulfillment from a cybernetic perspective: A new psychological theory of well-being. *Personality and Social Psychology Review: An Official Journal of the Society for Personality and Social Psychology, Inc*, 27(1), 3–27.

Dimeff, L. & Linehan, M. M. (2001). Dialectical behavior therapy in a nutshell. *The California Psychologist*, 34(3), 10–13.

Domschke, K., Stevens, S., Pfleiderer, B., & Gerlach, A. L. (2010). Interoceptive sensitivity in anxiety and anxiety disorders: An overview and integration of neurobiological findings. *Clinical Psychology Review*, 30(1), 1–11.

DSMTF & American Psychiatric Association. (2013). *Diagnostic and statistical manual of mental disorders: DSM-5* (Vol. 5, No. 5). American Psychiatric Association.

Dunn, B. D., Galton, H. C., Morgan, R. et al. (2010). Listening to your heart: How interoception shapes emotion experience and intuitive decision making. *Psychological Science*, 21(12), 1835–1844.

Ehlers, A., Breuer, P., Dohn, D., & Fiegenbaum, W. (1995). Heartbeat perception and panic disorder: Possible explanations for discrepant findings. *Behaviour Research and Therapy*, 33(1), 69–76.

Eickers, G. (forthcoming). *Ergo*.

Eickers, G., & Prinz, J. (2020). Emotion recognition as a social skill. In E. Fridland & C. Pavese, eds., *The Routledge handbook of philosophy of skill and expertise*. Routledge, pp. 347–361.

Ekman, P. E., & Davidson, R. J. (1994). *The nature of emotion: Fundamental questions*. Oxford University Press.

Elmas, H. G., Cesur, G., & Oral, E. T. (2017). Aleksitimi ve Patolojik Kumar: Duygu Düzenleme Güçlüğünün Aracı Rolü [Alexithymia and Pathological Gambling: The Mediating Role of Difficulties in Emotion Regulation]. *Turk psikiyatri dergisi = Turkish Journal of Psychiatry*, 28(1), 17–24.

Erbas, Y., Ceulemans, E., Kalokerinos, E. K. et al. (2018). Why I don't always know what I'm feeling: The role of stress in within-person fluctuations in emotion differentiation. *Journal of Personality and Social Psychology*, 115(2), 179–191.

Erbas, Y., Kalokerinos, E. K., Kuppens, P., van Halem, S., & Ceulemans, E. (2021). Momentary emotion differentiation: The derivation and validation of an index to study within-person fluctuations in emotion differentiation. *Assessment*, 29(4), 700–716. https://doi.org/10.1177/1073191121990089.

Ericsson, A. K. (2008). Deliberate practice and acquisition of expert performance: A general overview. *Academic Emergency Medicine*, 15(11), 988–994.

Feltovich, P., Prietula, M., & Ericsson, K. A. (2006). Studies of expertise from psychological perspectives. In K. A. Ericsson, ed., *The Cambridge Handbook of Expertise and Expert Performance*. Cambridge: Cambridge University Press, pp. 41–68.

Fischer, D., Messner, M., & Pollatos, O. (2017). Improvement of interoceptive processes after an 8-week body scan intervention. *Frontiers in Human Neuroscience*, 11, 452.

Fisher, J. (2019). Sensorimotor psychotherapy in the treatment of trauma. *Practice Innovations*, 4(3), 156.

Frewen, P. A., Dozois, D. J., Neufeld, R. W., & Lanius, R. A. (2008). Meta-analysis of alexithymia in posttraumatic stress disorder. *Journal of Traumatic Stress*, 21(2), 243–246.

Fridland, E. (2014). They've lost control: Reflections on skill. *Synthese*, 191(12), 2729–2750.

Fridland, E. (2017). Automatically minded. *Synthese*, 194, 4337–4363.

Fridland, E. (2019). Longer, smaller, faster, stronger: On skills and intelligence. *Philosophical Psychology*, 32(5), 759–783.

Fridland, E. (2020). The nature of skill: functions and control structures. In E. Fridland & C. Pavese, eds., *The Routledge handbook of philosophy of skill and expertise*. Routledge, pp. 245–257.

Fridland, E. (2021). Skill and strategic control. *Synthese*, 199(3–4), 5937–5964.

Fridland, E. & Stichter, M. (2021). It Just Feels Right: an account of expert intuition. *Synthese*, 199, 1327–1346.

Friedman, M. (1986). Autonomy and the split-level self. *The Southern Journal of Philosophy*, 24(1), 19–35.

Frijda, N. H. (1986). *The emotions*. Cambridge University Press.

Furman, D. J., Waugh, C. E., Bhattacharjee, K., Thompson, R. J., & Gotlib, I. H. (2013). Interoceptive awareness, positive affect, and decision making in major depressive disorder. *Journal of Affective Disorders*, 151(2), 780–785.

Füstös, J., Gramann, K., Herbert, B. M., & Pollatos, O. (2013). On the embodiment of emotion regulation: interoceptive awareness facilitates reappraisal. *Social Cognitive and Affective Neuroscience*, 8(8), 911–917.

Gilbert, P. (2010). *Compassion focused therapy: Distinctive features*. Routledge.

Goldie, P. (2002). Emotions, feelings and intentionality. *Phenomenology and the Cognitive Sciences*, 1(3), 235–254.

Goldie, P. (2004). Emotion, feeling, and knowledge of the world. In R. C. Solomon, ed., *Thinking about feeling: Contemporary philosophers on emotions*. Oxford University Press, pp. 91–106.

Griffiths, P. E., & Scarantino, A. (2005). Emotions in the wild: The situated perspective on emotion. In P. Robbins, ed., *The Cambridge handbook of situated cognition*. Cambridge University Press, pp. 437–453.

Gross, J. J., & John, O. P. (2003). Individual differences in two emotion regulation processes: Implications for affect, relationships, and well-being. *Journal of Personality and Social Psychology*, 85, 348–362.

Gross, J. J., & Thompson, R. A. (2007). Emotion Regulation: Conceptual Foundations. In J. J. Gross, ed., *Handbook of emotion regulation*. New York: Guilford Press, pp. 3–24.

Hayes, S. C., Strosahl, K. D., & Wilson, K. G. (2009). *Acceptance and commitment therapy*. American Psychological Association.

Hayes, S. C., Wilson, K. G., Gifford, E. V., Follette, V. M., & Strosahl, K. (1996). Experiential avoidance and behavioral disorders: A functional dimensional approach to diagnosis and treatment. *Journal of Consulting and Clinical Psychology*, 64(6), 1152–1168.

Herbert, B. M., Herbert, C., & Pollatos, O. (2011). On the relationship between interoceptive awareness and alexithymia: Is interoceptive awareness related to emotional awareness? *Journal of Personality*, 79(5), 1149–1175.

Herbert, B. M., & Pollatos, O. (2012). The body in the mind: on the relationship between interoception and embodiment. *Topics in Cognitive Science*, 4(4), 692–704.

Herbert, B. M., Ulbrich, P., & Schandry, R. (2007). Interoceptive sensitivity and physical effort: Implications for the self-control of physical load in everyday life. *Psychophysiology*, 44, 194–202.

Herman, J. L. (1992). *Trauma and recovery: From domestic abuse to political terror*. Basic Books.

Herwig, U., Kaffenberger, T., Jäncke, L., & Brühl, A. B. (2010). Self-related awareness and emotion regulation. *NeuroImage*, 50(2), 734–741.

Hoemann, K., Feldman Barrett, L., & Quigley, K. S. (2021). Emotional granularity increases with intensive ambulatory assessment: Methodological and individual factors influence how much. *Frontiers in Psychology*, 12, 1–13. https://doi.org/10.3389/fpsyg.2021.704125.

Hogeveen, J., & Grafman, J. (2021). Alexithymia. *Handbook of Clinical Neurology*, 183, 47–62.

Jäger, C. (2009). Affective ignorance. *Erkenntnis*, 71(1), 123–139.

Jaggar, A. M. (1989) Love and knowledge: Emotion in feminist epistemology, *Inquiry*, 32(2), 151–176

Jamieson, J. P., Hangen, E. J., Lee, H. Y., & Yeager, D. S. (2018). Capitalizing on appraisal processes to improve affective responses to social stress. *Emotion Review*, 10(1), 30–39.

Johnston, M. (2001). The authority of affect. *Philosophy and Phenomenological Research*, 63(1), 181–214.

Jones, K. (2003). Emotion, weakness of will, and the normative conception of agency. In A. Hatzimoysis, ed., *Philosophy and the Emotions*. Cambridge University Press. pp. 181–200.

Jongsma Jr, A. E., Peterson, L. M., & Bruce, T. (2021). *The complete adult psychotherapy treatment planner*. John Wiley & Sons.

Kashdan, T. B., Barrett, L. F., & McKnight, P. E. (2015). Unpacking emotion differentiation: Transforming unpleasant experience by perceiving distinctions in negativity. *Current Directions in Psychological Science*, 24(1), 10–16.

Kashdan, T. B., & Farmer, A. S. (2014). Differentiating emotions across contexts: Comparing adults with and without social anxiety disorder using random, social interaction, and daily experience sampling. *Emotion*, 14(3), 629–638.

Kashdan, T. B., Ferssizidis, P., Collins, R. L., & Muraven, M. (2010). Emotion differentiation as resilience against excessive alcohol use: An ecological momentary assessment in underage social drinkers. *Psychological Science*, 21(9), 1341–1347.

Khalsa, S. S., Adolphs, R., Cameron, O. G. et al. (2018). Interoception and mental health: A roadmap. *Biological Psychiatry: Cognitive Neuroscience and Neuroimaging*, 3(6), 501–13.

Khalsa, S. S., Craske, M. G., Li, W. et al. (2015). Altered interoceptive awareness in anorexia nervosa: Effects of meal anticipation, consumption and bodily arousal. *International Journal of Eating Disorders*, 48(7), 889–897.

Kinnaird, E., Stewart, C., & Tchanturia, K. (2019). Investigating alexithymia in autism: A systematic review and meta-analysis. *European Psychiatry: The Journal of the Association of European Psychiatrists*, 55, 80–89.

Koch, A., & Pollatos, O. (2014). Cardiac sensitivity in children: Sex differences and its relationship to parameters of emotional processing. *Psychophysiology*, 51(9), 932–941.

Kolnai, A. (1978). Deliberation is of ends. In Williams, B. and Wiggins, D. eds., *Ethics, Value and Reality, Selected Papers of Aurel Kolnai*, Indianapolis: Hackett, pp. 44–62.

Krauzlis, R. J., Bollimunta, A., Arcizet, F., & Wang, L. (2014). Attention as an effect not a cause. *Trends in Cognitive Sciences*, 18(9), 457–464.

Krauzlis, R. J., Wang, L., Yu, G., & Katz, L. N. (2023). What is attention?. *Wiley Interdisciplinary Reviews. Cognitive Science*, 14(1), e1570.

Latham, G. P., Brcic, J., & Steinhauer, A. (2017). Toward an integration of goal setting theory and the automaticity model. *Applied Psychology*, 66(1), 25–48.

LeDoux, J. E. (2000). Emotion circuits in the brain. *Annual Review of Neuroscience*, 23, 155–184.

Leeb, C. (2018a). Rebelling against suffering in capitalism. *Contemporary Political Theory*, 17(3), 263–282.

Leeb, C. (2018b). Rethinking embodied reflective judgment with Adorno and Arendt. *Constellations*, 25(3), 446–458.

Leweke, F., Leichsenring, F., Kruse, J., & Hermes, S. (2012) Is alexithymia associated with specific mental disorders? *Psychopathology*, 45, 22–28.

Lieberman, M. D., Eisenberger, N. I., Crockett, M. J. et al. (2007). Putting feelings into words: Affect labeling disrupts amygdala activity in response to affective stimuli. *Psychological Science*, 18(5), 421–428.

Lindahl, J. R., Fisher, N. E., Cooper, D. J., Rosen, R. K., & Britton, W. B. (2017). The varieties of contemplative experience: A mixed-methods study of meditation-related challenges in Western Buddhists. *PloS One*, 12(5), e0176239.

Lindquist, K., & Barrett, L. F. (2008). Emotional complexity. In M. Lewis, J. M. Haviland-Jones & L. F. Barrett, eds., *The handbook of emotion*, 3rd ed. New York: Guildford Press, pp. 513–530.

Maiese, M. (2014). How can emotions be both cognitive and bodily? *Phenomenology and the Cognitive Sciences*, 13, 513–531.

Maister, L. & Tsakiris, M. (2013). My face, my heart: Cultural differences in integrated bodily self-awareness. *Cognitive Neuroscience*, 5(1), 10–16.

Majeed, R. (2022). What not to make of recalcitrant emotions. *Erkenntnis*, 87, 747–765.

Mallon, R. & Stich, S. P. (2000). The odd couple: The compatibility of social construction and evolutionary psychology. *Philosophy of Science*, 67(1), 133–154.

Mendelovici, A. (2013). Intentionalism about moods. *Thought*, 2, 126–136.

Mesquita, B. (2022). *Between us: How cultures create emotions*. WW Norton.

Miller, J. B. (2012). *Toward a new psychology of women*. Beacon Press.

Millikan, R. G. (1995). Pushmi-pullyu representations. *Philosophical Perspectives*, 9, 185–200.

Moss, J. (2011). "Virtue makes the goal right": Virtue and phronesis in Aristotle's ethics. *Phronesis*, 56(3), 204–261.

Müller, J. M. (2017). How (not) to think of emotions as evaluative attitudes. *Dialectica*, 71(2), 281–308.

Nisbett, R. E. & Wilson, T. D. (1977). Telling more than we can know: Verbal reports on mental processes. *Psychological Review*, 84(3), 231–259.

Noë, A. (2004). *Action in perception*. MIT Press.

Nook, E. C., Sasse, S. F., Lambert, H. K., McLaughlin, K. A., & Somerville, L. H. (2018). The nonlinear development of emotion differentiation: Granular emotional experience is low in adolescence. *Psychological Science*, 29(8), 1346–1357.

Nussbaum, M. C. (2001). *Upheavals of thought: The intelligence of emotions*. Cambridge University Press.

O'Regan, J. K. (1992). Solving the "real" mysteries of visual perception: The world as an outside memory. *Canadian Journal of Psychology/Revue canadienne de psychologie*, 46(3), 461–488.

Ogden, P., Pain, C., & Fisher, J. (2006). A sensorimotor approach to the treatment of trauma and dissociation. *Psychiatric Clinics*, 29(1), 263–279.

Onur, E., Alkın, T., Sheridan, M. J., & Wise, T. N. (2013). Alexithymia and emotional intelligence in patients with panic disorder, generalized anxiety disorder and major depressive disorder. *The Psychiatric Quarterly*, 84(3), 303–311.

Ortony, A., Clore, G., & Collins, A. (1990). *The cognitive structure of emotions.* Cambridge University Press.

Parkinson, B. (2019). *Heart to heart.* Cambridge University Press.

Phan, K. L., & Sripada, C. S. (2013). Emotion regulation. In J. Armony & P. Vuilleumier, eds., *The Cambridge handbook of human affective neuroscience.* Cambridge University Press, pp. 375–400.

Pollatos, O., Kurz, A. L., Albrecht, J. et al. (2008). Reduced perception of bodily signals in anorexia nervosa. *Eating Behaviors*, 9(4), 381–388.

Pollatos, O., Traut-Mattausch, E., & Schandry, R. (2009). Differential effects of anxiety and depression on interoceptive accuracy. *Depression and Anxiety*, 26(2), 167–173.

Pond Jr, R. S., Kashdan, T. B., DeWall, C. N. et al. (2012). Emotion differentiation moderates aggressive tendencies in angry people: A daily diary analysis. *Emotion*, 12(2), 326–337.

Price, C. J., & Hooven, C. (2018). Interoceptive awareness skills for emotion regulation: Theory and approach of mindful awareness in body-oriented therapy (MABT). *Frontiers in Psychology*, 9, 798.

Prinz, J. J. (2004). *Gut reactions: A perceptual theory of emotion.* Oxford University Press.

Ridderinkhof, K. R. (2017). Emotion in action: A predictive processing perspective and theoretical synthesis. *Emotion Review*, 9(4), 319–325.

Roberts, R. C. (1995). Feeling one's emotions and knowing oneself. *Philosophical Studies: An International Journal for Philosophy in the Analytic Tradition*, 77(2/3), 319–338.

Roberts, R. C. (2003). *Emotions: An essay in aid of moral psychology.* Cambridge University Press.

Roberts, R. C. (2013). *Emotions in the moral life.* Cambridge University Press.

Rogers, C. R. (1995). *A way of being.* Houghton Mifflin Harcourt.

Rolla, G. (2018). Radical enactivism and self-knowledge. *Kriterion*, 141, 732–743.

Russell, J. A. (2003). Core affect and the psychological construction of emotion. *Psychological Review*, 110(1), 145–172.

Saul, J. (2013). Scepticism and implicit bias. *Disputatio*, 5(37), 243–263.

Scherer, K. R., & Moors, A. (2019). The emotion process: Event appraisal and component differentiation. *Annual Review of Psychology*, 70, 719–745.

Schirmer-Mokwa, K. L., Fard, P. R., Zamorano, A. M. et al. (2015). Evidence for enhanced interoceptive accuracy in professional musicians. *Frontiers in Behavioral Neuroscience*, 9, 1–13.

Schultheiss, O. C., & Brunstein, J. C. (1999). Goal imagery: Bridging the gap between implicit motives and explicit goals. *Journal of Personality*, 67(1), 1–38.

Schultheiss, O. C., & Strasser, A. (2012). Referential processing and competence as determinants of congruence between implicit and explicit motives. In S. Vazire & T. D. Wilson, eds., *Handbook of self-knowledge*. The Guilford Press, pp. 39–62.

Schwarz, N. (2011). Feelings-as-information theory. *Handbook of Theories of Social Psychology*, 1, 289–308.

Schwitzgebel, E. (2008). The unreliability of naive introspection. *Philosophical Review*, 117(2), 245–273.

Schwitzgebel, E. (2012). Self-ignorance. In J. Liu & J. Perry, eds., *Consciousness and the self: New essays*. Cambridge University Press, pp. 184–197.

Selby, E., Wonderlich, S. A., Crosby, R. D., et al. (2014). Nothing Tastes as Good as Thin Feels: Low Positive Emotion Differentiation and Weight-Loss Activities in Anorexia Nervosa. *Clinical Psychological Science*, 2(4), 514–531.

Shargel, D. & Prinz, J. J. (2018). An enactivist theory of emotional content. In H. Naar & F. Teroni, eds., *The ontology of emotions*. Cambridge University Press, pp. 110–129.

Sheppes, G., Scheibe, S., Suri, G., & Gross, J. J. (2011). Emotion-regulation choice. *Psychological Science*, 22(11), 1391–1396.

Sheppes, G., Scheibe, S., Suri, G., Radu, P., Blechert, J., & Gross, J. J. (2014). Emotion regulation choice: A conceptual framework and supporting evidence. *Journal of Experimental Psychology: General*, 143(1), 163–181.

Shipko, S., Alvarez, W. A., & Noviello, N. (1983). Towards a teleological model of alexithymia: Alexithymia and post-traumatic stress disorder. *Psychotherapy and Psychosomatics*, 39(2), 122–126.

Silva, L. (2021). The epistemic role of outlaw emotions. *Ergo an Open Access Journal of Philosophy*, 8, 23.

Simon, G. E., Shortreed, S. M., Rossom, R. C. et al. (2022). Effect of offering care management or online dialectical behavior therapy skills training vs usual care on self-harm among adult outpatients with suicidal ideation: A randomized clinical trial. *JAMA*, 327(7), 630–638.

Slaby, J. (2008). Affective intentionality and the feeling body. *Phenomenology and the Cognitive Sciences*, 7(4), 429–444.

Solomon, R. C. (1980). Emotions and choice. In A. O. Rorty, ed., *Explaining emotions*. University of California Press, pp. 251–281.

Sosa, E. (2007). *A virtue epistemology: Apt belief and reflective knowledge, Volume 1*. Oxford University Press.

Sosniak, L. A. (1987). The nature of change in successful learning. *Teachers College Record*, 88(4), 519–535.

Sreenivasan, G. (2018). Emotions, reasons, and epistemology. *Philosophy and Phenomenological Research*, 97(2), 500–506.

Starkey, C. (2008). Emotions and full understanding. *Ethical Theory and Moral Practice*, 11(4), 425–454.

Stasiewicz, P. R., Bradizza, C. M., Gudleski, G. D., et al. (2012) The relationship of alexithymia to emotional dysregulation within an alcohol dependent treatment sample. *Addictive Behaviors*, 37, 469–476.

Stephan, A. (2017). Moods in Layers. *Philosophia*, 45, 1481–1495.

Stichter, M. (2018). *The skillfulness of virtue: Improving our moral and epistemic lives*. Cambridge University Press.

Stichter, M. (2020). Learning from failure: Shame and emotion regulation in virtue as skill. *Ethical Theory and Moral Practice*, 23, 341–354.

Stichter, M. (2024). Flourishing goals, metacognitive skills, and the virtue of wisdom. *Topoi*.

Suvak, M. K., Litz, B. T., Sloan, D. M. et al. (2011). Emotional granularity and borderline personality disorder. *Journal of Abnormal Psychology*, 120(2), 414–426.

Tappolet, C. (2000). *Émotions et valeurs*. Presses Universitaires France.

Tappolet, C. (2016). *Emotions, values, and agency*. Oxford University Press.

Taylor, J. G., & Fragopanagos, N. F. (2005). The interaction of attention and emotion. *Neural Networks: The Official Journal of the International Neural Network Society*, 18(4), 353–369.

Terasawa, Y., Moriguchi, Y., Tochizawa, S., & Umeda, S. (2014). Interoceptive sensitivity predicts sensitivity to the emotions of others. *Cognition and Emotion*, 28(8), 1435–1448.

Terhaar, J., Viola, F. C., Bär, K. J., & Debener, S. (2012). Heartbeat evoked potentials mirror altered body perception in depressed patients. *Clinical Neurophysiology*, 123(10), 1950–1957.

Teroni, F. (2007). Emotions and formal objects. *Dialectica*, 61(3), 395–415.

Thompson, R. J., Springstein, T., & Boden, M. (2021). Gaining clarity about emotion differentiation. *Social and Personality Psychology Compass*, 15(3), Article e12584.

References

Tiberius, V., & DeYoung, C. (2022). Pain, depression, and goal-fulfillment theories of ill-being. *Midwest Studies in Philosophy*, 46, 165–191.

Tomko, R. L., Lane, S. P., Pronove, L. M. et al. (2015). Undifferentiated negative affect and impulsivity in borderline personality and depressive disorders: A momentary perspective. *Journal of Abnormal Psychology*, 124(3), 740–753.

Van der Gucht, K., Dejonckheere, E., Erbas, Y. et al. (2019). An experience sampling study examining the potential impact of a mindfulness-based intervention on emotion differentiation. *Emotion*, 19(1), 123–131.

Van der Kolk, B. A. (1994). The body keeps the score: Memory and the evolving psychobiology of posttraumatic stress. *Harvard Review of Psychiatry*, 1(5), 253–265.

Vedernikova, E., Kuppens, P., & Erbas, Y. (2021). From knowledge to differentiation: Increasing emotion knowledge through an intervention increases negative emotion differentiation. *Frontiers in Psychology*, 12, Article 703757.

Widdershoven, R. L., Wichers, M., Kuppens, P. et al. (2019). Effect of self-monitoring through experience sampling on emotion differentiation in depression. *Journal of Affective Disorders*, 244, 71–77.

Williamson, T. (2000). *Knowledge and its limits*. Oxford University Press.

Wu, W. (2011). Attention as Selection for Action. In C. Mole, D. Smithies & W. Wu, eds., *Attention: Philosophical and psychological essays*. New York: Oxford University Press. pp. 97–116.

Wu, W. (2024). We know what attention is!. *Trends in Cognitive Sciences* 28(4), 304–318.

Zaki, J., Davis, J. I., & Ochsner, K. N. (2012). Overlapping activity in anterior insula during interoception and emotional experience. *Neuroimage*, 62(1), 493–499.

Zeitlin, S. B., & McNally, R. J. (1993). Alexithymia and anxiety sensitivity in panic disorder and obsessive-compulsive disorder. *American Journal of Psychiatry*, 150, 658–660.

Cambridge Elements

Epistemology

Stephen Hetherington
University of New South Wales, Sydney

Stephen Hetherington is Professor Emeritus of Philosophy at the University of New South Wales, Sydney. He is the author of numerous books, including *Knowledge and the Gettier Problem* (Cambridge University Press, 2016), and *What Is Epistemology?* (Polity, 2019), and is the editor of several others, including *Knowledge in Contemporary Epistemology* (with Markos Valaris: Bloomsbury, 2019), and *What the Ancients Offer to Contemporary Epistemology* (with Nicholas D. Smith: Routledge, 2020). He was the Editor-in-Chief of the Australasian Journal of Philosophy from 2013 until 2022.

About the Series

This Elements series seeks to cover all aspects of a rapidly evolving field, including emerging and evolving topics such as: fallibilism; knowing how; self-knowledge; knowledge of morality; knowledge and injustice; formal epistemology; knowledge and religion; scientific knowledge; collective epistemology; applied epistemology; virtue epistemology; wisdom. The series demonstrates the liveliness and diversity of the field, while also pointing to new areas of investigation.

Cambridge Elements

Epistemology

Elements in the Series

Higher-Order Evidence and Calibrationism
Ru Ye

The Nature and Normativity of Defeat
Christoph Kelp

Philosophy, Bullshit, and Peer Review
Neil Levy

Stratified Virtue Epistemology: A Defence
J. Adam Carter

The Skeptic and the Veridicalist: On the Difference Between Knowing What There Is and Knowing What Things Are
Yuval Avnur

Transcendental Epistemology
Tony Cheng

Knowledge and God
Matthew A. Benton

Knowing What It Is Like
Yuri Cath

Disagreement
Diego E. Machuca

On Believing and Being Convinced
Paul Silva Jr

Knowledge-First Epistemology: A Defence
Mona Simion

Emotional Self-Knowledge: How Affective Skills Reveal Our Values, Goals, Cares, and Concerns
Matt Stichter and Ellen Fridland

A full series listing is available at: www.cambridge.org/EEPI

For EU product safety concerns, contact us at Calle de José Abascal, 56–1º,
28003 Madrid, Spain or eugpsr@cambridge.org.

www.ingramcontent.com/pod-product-compliance
Ingram Content Group UK Ltd.
Pitfield, Milton Keynes, MK11 3LW, UK
UKHW021930220625
459989UK00014B/93